CRISIS AS CATALYST - BUILDING TEAMS THROUGH CHALLENGES

WHY TRADITIONAL TEAM ACTIVITIES FALL SHORT AND HOW TO FORGE UNBREAKABLE BONDS

RANABIR ROY

Contents

Preface

The journey of writing this book began with a simple yet profound observation: in moments of crisis, we often see the true potential of individuals and teams. As a senior leader in the software industry, I have witnessed firsthand how crises can either fracture teams or forge them into more resilient and cohesive units. The difference lies not just in the nature of the crisis but in how it is managed and, more importantly, how it is perceived by those involved.

In today's fast-paced, ever-changing world, crises are inevitable. Whether it's a technical failure, a market downturn, or an internal conflict, challenges will arise. Yet, these challenges also present opportunities—opportunities to build stronger teams, to drive innovation, and to reinforce a shared sense of purpose. This book is about harnessing the power of those opportunities and turning crisis into catalysts for growth and team building.

As I reflected on my experiences and those of my peers, it became clear that traditional team-building exercises, while valuable in certain contexts, often fall short in preparing teams for real-world challenges. Activities like team outings or workshops can foster camaraderie to some extent, but they rarely test the mettle of a team in the way that a true crisis does. It is in the heat of a crisis that the strengths, weaknesses, and true character of a team are revealed.

This realization led me to explore the concept of crisis-driven team building more deeply. Through extensive research, interviews with industry leaders, and analysis of historical events, I sought to uncover the principles and practices that can help leaders turn crisis into powerful opportunities for team development. The result is a collection of insights, strategies, and real-world examples that illustrate how effective leadership can transform a crisis from a threat into a unifying force.

One of the key themes of this book is the psychological impact of crises on teams and individuals. Understanding how people respond to stress, uncertainty, and high-pressure situations is crucial for leaders who wish to guide their teams through difficult times. By exploring these psychological dynamics, I aim to equip leaders with the tools they need to support their teams, maintain morale, and foster a sense of collective resilience.

Another important focus of this book is the role of leadership in creating a culture of continuous learning and adaptation. In a world where the only constant is change, the ability to learn from past experiences, adapt to new challenges, and innovate in response to crises is essential for long-term success. This book offers practical advice on how to cultivate this mindset within your team, ensuring that you are not only prepared for the next crisis but are also positioned to emerge from it stronger than before.

Throughout the book, I have included real stories of leaders who have successfully navigated crises, drawing from both my own experiences and those of others across various industries. These stories serve as powerful examples of how crisis-driven team building can lead to remarkable outcomes. They also provide valuable lessons that can be applied to your own leadership journey.

Writing this book has been a deeply rewarding experience, one that has allowed me to reflect on the challenges and triumphs of my own career while also learning from the experiences of others. My hope is that the insights and strategies shared in these pages will inspire you to embrace crises as opportunities for growth and to lead your teams with confidence, clarity, and compassion.

I am deeply grateful to all my colleagues, mentors, and leaders who have shared their stories and insights with me, that has contributed to the richness of this book. Their experiences have not only informed the content but have also reinforced my belief in the power of crisis-driven team building.

As you read this book, I encourage you to think about the challenges you have faced as a leader and the opportunities that lie ahead. How can you turn the next crisis into a moment of transformation for your team? How can you leverage the lessons of the past to build a more resilient and cohesive team in the future?

In closing, I would like to thank you for choosing this book and for your commitment to become a more effective leader. Leadership is not a destination but a continuous journey of growth and learning. I hope that this book serves as a valuable resource on your journey, helping you to navigate the complexities of leadership in a world where crises are not only inevitable but also invaluable.

With sincere appreciation,

Ranabir Roy

Introduction

The Traditional Approach to Team Building

In today's corporate world, particularly in industries such as Information Technology and Software Development, the cohesion of a team is essential for success. A team's ability to collaborate, trust each other and operate as a unified entity can make the difference between a " project's success or failure". While traditional wisdom suggests that team outings, retreats and similar activities are the best ways to build these bonds, they often provide only temporary relief from the day-to-day work and do not foster the deep, lasting connections needed to thrive in the complex and high-pressure environments of these industries.

This introduction explores the psychological differences between team bonding during leisurely outings and the deeper connections that are often formed in the midst of crisis. We will investigate why conventional team-building methods tend to be ineffective and how crisis can serve as powerful drivers for creating stronger and more resilient teams. Throughout this section, I will illustrate these ideas with real-life examples, highlighting the experiences of Indian and global leaders, as well as corporate stories that uncover the authentic dynamics of team building.

The Psychology of Team Outings

Team outings are a common practice in corporate culture. They are designed to be enjoyable, casual experiences where team members can unwind, bond with each other outside the workplace, and foster camaraderie. The underlying idea is that these outings will contribute to improved teamwork and communication in the office.

From a psychological standpoint, team outings operate based on the concept of social facilitation. This theory suggests that individuals tend to perform better on simple tasks when they are in the presence of others. In the context of a team outing, this means that team members are likely to engage in more positive, cooperative behaviors because they are in an environment that encourages these behaviors. The informal setting of an outing, such as a day at a resort or a team dinner, breaks down the hierarchical barriers present in the office and allows individuals to interact more freely.

However, this setting also has its limitations. The relaxed atmosphere may foster connections, but it does not necessarily mimic the pressures or challenges of the workplace. Team members may get along well during a casual game of cricket or a karaoke night, but these interactions are often superficial. The bonding formed in such environments may not be strong enough to withstand the stress and complexity of real work challenges.

Consider the story of a Bangalore-based software company that organized a weekend retreat in Coorg. The team spent the weekend participating in adventure sports, playing games and enjoying bonfires. During the retreat, everyone seemed to get along well and there was a sense of camaraderie among the team members. However, when they returned to the office, the same old issues—miscommunication, lack of trust and unclear roles—began to surface again. The retreat had provided a temporary break, but it had not addressed the underlying problems within the team.

This example highlights a key limitation of team outings: they foster a temporary sense of unity that often fades once the team returns to the pressures of their work environment. The connections formed during these outings are often superficial, as they are built in a context that does not mirror the true nature of the challenges the team faces.

The Crisis-Driven Approach

In contrast to the informal setting of a team outing, crisis brings out a different side of human psychology. Crises are high-pressure events that require immediate action, clear communication and strong leadership. The stakes are higher and the environment is often unpredictable. In such situations, the superficial layers of behavior that people exhibit during more relaxed interactions are stripped away, revealing their true character and capabilities.

Psychologically, crisis triggers the fight-or-flight response, a survival mechanism that prepares individuals to either confront or flee from a threat. In a team setting, this response can lead to heightened awareness, increased focus and a stronger sense of solidarity among team members. When faced with a common threat, individuals are more likely to put aside their differences and work together to find a solution.

One powerful example of this dynamic can be found in the story of the Indian Space Research Organisation (ISRO) during the Chandrayaan-2 mission. In 2019, the mission's Vikram lander lost communication with Earth during its descent to the moon. The entire ISRO team, from the top scientists to the engineers on the ground, were thrust into a crisis situation. Despite the immense pressure, the team worked tirelessly to analyze the situation and salvage the mission. Though the lander ultimately failed to make a soft landing, the crisis brought the team closer together. The shared experience of working through such a high-stake situation forged a bond amongst the team members that was far deeper than anything that could have been achieved through a team outing or a retreat.

This example illustrates how a crisis can bring out the best in a team. The urgency and intensity of a crisis can force team members to collaborate in ways that they might not in a more relaxed setting. The bonding formed in such situations are often stronger and more enduring because they are based on shared experiences of overcoming adversity.

Why This Book?

This book is for leaders who want to build resilient, high-performing teams. It's for those who have tried traditional team-building activities and found them lacking. It's for those who understand that the true test of a team's strength comes not in moments of relaxation but during a crisis.

The idea of this book stems from my own experiences in the Information Technology (IT) industry. Throughout my 19-years career, I've seen teams come together and fall apart during challenges. I've witnessed how crises can either break a team or transform it into something extraordinary.

One of the most profound lessons I've learned is that a crisis, when managed effectively, can be a powerful opportunity for team building. However, this requires a different mindset for both leaders and team members. It requires seeing crises not as threats, but as opportunities to foster growth, innovation and unity.

I've had the privilege of working with incredible teams in companies like Kyocera Wireless, Samsung, Amazon and Hinge Health. In each of these environments, I've seen how teams respond to crises and I've gathered countless stories and insights that I'm eager to share with you.

This book will draw on a range of examples—from ancient Indian Epics ,the Ramayana and Mahabharata to modern-day leaders and sports personalities. These stories will illustrate the power of crisis-driven team building and provide practical insights that you can apply in your organization.

Whether you're a manager, a senior leader or an aspiring leader, this book will equip you with the tools and strategies you need to turn crises into opportunities for team bonding and growth. At the end of this journey, you'll have a new perspective on leadership, one that embraces challenges and sees them as the crucible in which great teams are forged.

The Flaws of Traditional Team Building

Traditional team-building activities like outings, workshops and games are meant to foster team bonding, but they often fail to address the root issues affecting team performance. These activities take place in artificial settings removed from the workplace reality and tend to focus on surface-level interactions rather than the real challenges faced by teams.

One major issue with traditional team building is that it can create a sense of cognitive dissonance amongst team members. This occurs when there is a mismatch between their experience in one context and the reality they know to be true in another. For example, a team might bond during a fun outing, only to find that communication problems and lack of trust still exist when they return to the office, leading to frustration and disappointment.

A specific example of this is seen in a Mumbai-based startup that organized team-building workshops. Despite feeling more connected to their colleagues during the workshops, the team's underlying issues of poor leadership and unclear job roles still remained unaddressed, causing the same problems to persist afterward.

This illustrates the limitations of traditional team-building activities, which offer only temporary morale boosts without providing lasting solutions to teams' challenges. These activities are artificial and fail to replicate the demands of the work environment, resulting in surface-level bonds that do not translate into improved team performance.

A Story of Misalignment

To further illustrate the flaws of traditional team building, let's consider a real story of misalignment from an Indian multinational corporation. The company, which we'll call TechGlobal for confidentiality, was experiencing issues with collaboration and communication amongst its global teams. To address these issues, the management decided to organize a team-building retreat at a luxury resort in Goa.

The retreat included a variety of activities designed to promote teamwork, such as group games, trust exercises and team challenges. The participants enjoyed the retreat and felt that it had helped them get to know their colleagues better. However, when they returned to their respective offices, the same old issues of misalignment and miscommunication had resurfaced.

The problem was that the retreat had focused on surface-level interactions and had not addressed the deeper issues of cultural differences, unclear roles and lack of effective communication channels. The retreat had created a temporary sense of unity, but it had not provided the tools or frameworks needed to resolve the real challenges that the team actually faced.

This story highlights a critical flaw in traditional team-building methods: they often fail to address the root causes of team dysfunction. While these activities can provide a temporary boost in morale, they do not offer long-term solutions to the challenges that teams face. The activities are artificial and do not replicate the realities of the workplace, leading to a disconnect between the team-building experience and the actual work environment.

The Power of Crisis-Driven Team Building

In contrast to traditional methods, crisis-driven team building is rooted in real-world challenges. When a team is faced with a crisis, they are forced to confront their problems head-on. There's no time for pretense or avoidance; everyone must pull together to find a solution. This creates a sense of urgency and accountability that is often missing in traditional team-building activities.

The psychological concept of group cohesiveness is particularly relevant here. In a crisis, the need for cooperation and mutual support becomes paramount.

Team members are more likely to set aside their differences and work together towards a common goal. The shared experience of overcoming adversity can create a deep sense of trust and loyalty that is difficult to achieve through other means.

One powerful example of crisis-driven team building comes from the Indian Army. During the Kargil War in 1999, Indian soldiers were tasked with recapturing strategic peaks that had been occupied by enemy forces. The terrain was treacherous and the conditions were harsh. However, the soldiers displayed extraordinary teamwork, bravery and resilience. The bonding formed during this crisis was so strong that many soldiers reported feeling a deep sense of brotherhood with their comrades, a bond that endured long after the war was over. This is a prime example of how a crisis can bring a team together in a way that no amount of recreational activity ever could.

In the corporate world, a similar example can be found in the story of Tata Group during the 2008 Mumbai attacks. The Taj Mahal Palace Hotel, owned by the Tata Group, was one of the main targets of the terrorist attacks. In the aftermath, the employees of the hotel displayed extraordinary courage and dedication, with many risking their lives to save guests. The crisis brought the entire Tata Group together, reinforcing their commitment to their values and mission. The employees who went through this crisis emerged stronger and more united, with a deep sense of loyalty to the organization.

A Story from the Battlefield: The Siege of Lanka

One of the most powerful examples of crisis-driven team building came from the ancient Indian epic, the Ramayana.

The story of the Siege of Lanka offered timeless lessons on leadership, teamwork and resilience in the face of overwhelming odds.

In the Ramayana, Lord Rama's wife, Sita, was kidnapped by the demon king Ravana and taken to Lanka. To rescue her, Rama had to assemble an army and launch a siege on Ravana's fortress. The situation was dire—Ravana was a powerful ruler with a formidable army and Lanka was a heavily fortified island. The odds were stacked against Rama and his allies.

Despite the challenges, Rama was able to unite a diverse group of allies, including the monkey king Sugriva, the bear king Jambavan and the valiant warrior Hanuman. These allies came from different backgrounds and had different strengths, but they were united by a common goal: to rescue Sita and defeat Ravana.

The Siege of Lanka was a story of how a group of individuals, each with their unique skills and perspectives, came together to overcome a seemingly insurmountable challenge. The crisis forced them to work together in ways they never had before and it was through this collaboration that they were able to achieve victory.

This story illustrates a key principle of crisis-driven team building: when faced with a significant challenge, a team's differences can become its greatest strength. The shared experience of navigating a crisis not only strengthened the bonds between team members but also helped them discover new ways of working together.

Crisis-Driven Team Building vs. Traditional Methods

When comparing crisis-driven team building with traditional methods, the differences are striking. Traditional methods are often based on creating a positive and enjoyable environment for team members to bond. However, this approach can be superficial and does not always translate into improved team performance.

On the other hand, crisis-driven team building is based on real challenges and high stakes. It forces team members to confront their fears, push their limits and work together in ways they might not have thought possible. The bonds formed in such situations are often deeper and more enduring because they are based on shared experiences of overcoming adversity.

The psychology behind this is rooted in the concept of experiential learning, where individuals learn best through direct experience. In a crisis, team members are not just talking about working together—they are doing it. This hands-on experience creates a powerful sense of achievement and reinforces the importance of teamwork in a way that no theoretical discussion or recreational activity ever could.

The Purpose of This Book

The purpose of this book is to equip leaders with the tools and strategies they need to turn crisis into opportunities for team building and success. Whether you're facing a financial crisis, a technical challenge or a market disruption, the principles in this book will help you navigate the storm and emerge stronger on the other side.

Throughout this book, we'll explore a range of real-world examples, drawing from ancient texts, modern leaders and personal experiences. We'll look at how different types of crises—whether they be internal conflicts, external threats or unforeseen challenges—can be leveraged to build stronger, more cohesive teams.

You'll learn how to create a culture that embraces challenges, fosters collaboration and aligns with your company's mission and vision. You'll discover practical strategies for leading your team through crises, from setting clear goals and expectations to providing the tools and support they need to succeed.

By the time you finish reading the book , you'll have a new perspective on leadership and team building—one that sees crises not as obstacles but as opportunities for growth and transformation. Whether you're a seasoned leader or just starting out, this book will provide you with the insights and strategies you need to build strong, resilient teams that thrive in the face of adversity.

Looking Ahead

As we move forward, we'll dive deeper into the specific strategies and examples that illustrate the power of crisis-driven team building. We'll explore the role of leadership in navigating crises, the importance of aligning teams with your company's mission and vision and the lessons we can learn from ancient texts and modern leaders.

Each chapter will build on the concepts introduced here, providing you with a comprehensive guide to turning crisis into opportunities for team bonding and success. Whether you're leading a small team or a large organization, the principles in this book will help you harness the power of crises to build stronger, more cohesive teams.

So, let's embark on this journey together. Let's explore how crisis can be the catalyst for building teams that not only survive but thrive in the face of adversity. By embracing challenges and turning them into opportunities, you can create a team that is not just good but great—a team that is united, resilient and driven by a shared sense of purpose.

Let's get started.

Understanding Team Dynamics

In any organization, the success of a project or initiative hinges on the ability of a team to work together effectively. But what exactly makes a team work well? The answer lies in understanding the complex dynamics that underpin how individuals interact within a group. These dynamics determine how teams communicate, make decisions, resolve conflicts and ultimately, achieve their goals.

This chapter will explore the core elements of team dynamics, using real-world examples and stories to illustrate the principles that contribute to a team's success—or failure.

What Makes a Team?

A team is more than just a group of people working together. It's a collective of individuals who share a common purpose and are committed to achieving a specific goal. While the idea of a team might seem straightforward, the dynamics that govern how teams function are anything but simple.

1.1.1 The Foundation: Trust and Communication

The heart of any successful team is trust. Trust is the foundation upon which all other team dynamics are built. Without trust, communication breaks down, collaboration becomes difficult and the team's effectiveness is compromised.

The Rise of Google's Project Aristotle

In 2012, Google launched a research project called Project Aristotle, aimed at understanding what makes a team effective. The project involved analyzing hundreds of Google's teams to identify the key factors that contributed to their success. What the researchers found was surprising: the most successful teams weren't necessarily those with the best individual performers. Instead, the most effective teams were those that exhibited high levels of trust.

Google's researchers discovered that psychological safety—defined as a shared belief that the team is safe for interpersonal risk-taking—was the most critical factor in team success. In teams with high psychological safety, members felt comfortable being themselves, expressing their ideas, and admitting mistakes without fear of judgment or retribution.

The lesson from Project Aristotle is clear: trust and psychological safety are essential for a team's success. When team members trust each other, they are more likely to communicate openly, share ideas and collaborate effectively.

1.1.2 Communication: The Lifeblood of a Team

Communication is the vehicle through which trust is built and maintained. Effective communication involves more than just sharing information; it's about ensuring that everyone in the team is on the same page, understands the goals, and feels heard.

The Collapse of the Hyatt Regency Walkway

A tragic example of how poor communication and organizational misalignment can lead to disaster is the Hyatt Regency walkway collapse in Kansas City, Missouri, in 1981. This incident remains one of the deadliest structural failures in U.S. history, claiming the lives of 114 people and injuring over 200 others.

Background

The Hyatt Regency Hotel in Kansas City was a prestigious project, boasting a stunning design that included a multi-story atrium with suspended walkways connecting various floors. These walkways were architectural marvels meant to be both functional and aesthetically pleasing. However, beneath the surface, there were significant issues related to the construction and design of these walkways.

The Design Flaw

The original design for the walkways called for them to be suspended from the atrium ceiling using long steel rods. However, during construction, a change was made to the design to simplify the installation process. Instead of using a single continuous rod, the design was altered to use two shorter rods, with the lower walkway suspended from the upper one. This seemingly minor change had catastrophic implications. The new design doubled the load on the connection points of the upper walkway, something that was neither recognized nor calculated by the engineers at the time.

The Communication Breakdown

The change in design was communicated informally between the construction company and the engineering firm but the implications of this change were never fully understood or analyzed. The structural engineers failed to recognize the increased load that the new design would place on the walkways. Moreover, the communication between the construction team and the engineers was lacking in detail, with critical design documents not being updated to reflect the change.

Adding to the complexity, the hierarchical and fragmented nature of the project management structure meant that different teams were working in silos. Engineers, contractors and project managers were not on the same page, and there was no effective mechanism in place to ensure that changes were reviewed and approved at the necessary levels. The engineers assumed that the contractors would alert them if the change was problematic, while the contractors assumed that the engineers had already done the necessary calculations.

The Catastrophe

On the evening of July 17, 1981, during a tea dance event that attracted a large crowd to the atrium, the load on the walkways exceeded their structural capacity. The connection points failed, and the upper walkway collapsed onto the lower one, which then crashed down into the crowded atrium below.

The disaster was immediate and devastating. Emergency responders faced the gruesome task of rescuing the injured and recovering the bodies of those who had been killed. The aftermath revealed not just a physical collapse, but also a catastrophic failure in communication, decision-making and responsibility.

Lessons Learned

The Hyatt Regency walkway collapse serves as a stark reminder of the importance of clear, thorough communication and accountability in complex projects. In this case, a lack of communication and failure to follow rigorous review processes led to a design flaw being overlooked, with deadly consequences.

Had the engineering team and contractors communicated more effectively and had the design change undergone proper review and approval, the disaster could have been averted. This incident underscores the critical need for teams to work collaboratively, ensure that all changes are properly assessed, and maintain an open environment where concerns can be raised and addressed.

In any project, particularly those involving high stakes and complex systems, it is vital that every team member feels empowered to speak up, that communication channels are clear and open, and that decisions are made with a full understanding of their implications. The Hyatt Regency disaster teaches us that when these elements are missing, the consequences can be disastrous.

1.1.3 Collaboration: The Power of Working Together

While trust and communication are foundational, collaboration is the action that brings a team's efforts to life. Collaboration involves working together to achieve a common goal, leveraging the diverse skills, experiences and perspectives of each team member.

The Success of the Human Genome Project

The Human Genome Project (HGP), an international research initiative launched in 1990, aimed to map the entire human genome. This massive undertaking involved scientists from 20 institutions across six countries, working together to decode the 3 billion DNA base pairs that make up human genetics.

What made the HGP successful was the high level of collaboration among its participants. Scientists from different backgrounds, disciplines and institutions shared data, resources and findings freely, driven by the shared goal of advancing human knowledge.

The project's collaborative approach was key to its success. By working together and pooling their expertise, the researchers were able to complete the project ahead of schedule and under budget. The HGP is a testament to the power of collaboration and the incredible results that can be achieved when teams work together towards a common goal.

The Role of Individual Differences

While collaboration is essential, it's important to recognize that teams are made up of individuals, each with their strengths, weaknesses, personalities and working style. Understanding and managing these individual differences is a critical aspect of team dynamics.

1.2.1 The Importance of Diversity

Diversity within a team can be a double-edged sword. On one hand, diverse teams bring a range of perspectives and ideas, which can lead to more innovative solutions. On the other hand, diversity can also lead to misunderstandings and conflicts if not managed effectively.

Tata Motors and the Creation of the Nano: A Story of Diverse Perspectives

Tata Motors, one of India's leading automobile manufacturers, embarked on a groundbreaking project in the mid-2000s: the creation of the Tata Nano, a car that would be affordable to millions of Indians who previously could only dream of owning a vehicle. This ambitious project brought together a diverse team of engineers, designers and executives, all with different backgrounds, experiences and perspectives.

The Vision and the Challenge

The idea for the Tata Nano was born out of Ratan Tata's vision to create a "people's car" that would cost just ?1 lakh (about $2,000 at the time). Ratan Tata, the chairman of Tata Motors, wanted to address the safety and mobility needs of Indian families who often travelled on two-wheelers, sometimes carrying more passengers that was not safe. The challenge was immense: how to design, engineer and manufacture a car at such a low cost without compromising on quality and safety.

The Diverse Team Behind the Nano

To achieve this vision, Tata Motors assembled a team that was as diverse as the challenges they faced. The team included experienced automotive engineers from Tata Motors' plants in Pune and Lucknow, young designers from the company's design studios in Italy, and supply chain experts from various parts of India. Additionally, consultants from Germany and the United States were brought in to provide insights into global best practices in manufacturing and design.

This diversity in the team's composition was both a strength and a challenge. The engineers in India were deeply familiar with the needs and preferences of the Indian consumer, understanding the importance of affordability, fuel efficiency, and durability in the harsh Indian road conditions. The designers from Italy, on the other hand, brought with them a focus on aesthetics and innovation, while the consultants from abroad pushed for the integration of advanced engineering techniques and global standards.

The Clashes and Misunderstandings

As the team worked on the project, differences in working styles and priorities began to emerge. The Indian engineers were focused on cost-cutting measures, looking for ways to reduce the number of components and simplify the design to meet the aggressive price target. Meanwhile, the Italian designers were advocating for a stylish and modern look, which sometimes conflicted with the cost-saving goals. The global consultants, while bringing valuable expertise, often found themselves at odds with the local team's approach to problem-solving.

One particular incident exemplifies the challenges the team faced. The Italian designers proposed a more sophisticated suspension system that would improve the car's handling and ride quality. However, the Indian engineers quickly pointed out that this design would significantly increase the cost of production, making it impossible to meet the ?1 lakh price target. The ensuing discussions were tense, with both sides struggling to find common ground.

The Turning Point

Recognizing that the project was at risk of being derailed by these internal conflicts, Ratan Tata intervened. He emphasized the importance of the project's core mission: to create an affordable car for the masses. He encouraged the team to focus on the end goal and to leverage their diverse perspectives to find innovative solutions rather than allowing their differences to become obstacles.

The team responded by working more collaboratively. The engineers and designers began to engage in more open dialogues, seeking to understand each other's concerns and priorities. They also involved the global consultants in these discussions, ensuring that all viewpoints were considered in the decision-making process. This shift in approach led to several breakthroughs, including a redesign of the suspension system that balanced both cost and performance and innovative manufacturing techniques that reduced production costs without compromising quality.

The Launch of the Tata Nano

In 2008, Tata Motors launched the Tata Nano to great fanfare. While the car received mixed reviews and faced some market challenges, it remains a landmark in automotive history as the world's most affordable car. The project demonstrated how a diverse team when effectively managed and aligned with a common goal, can overcome significant challenges to achieve something truly remarkable.

1.2.2 Understanding Personality Types

Another important aspect of individual differences is personality. Different personality types can influence how team members interact, make decisions, and handle conflict. Understanding these differences can help teams work more effectively together.

The Infosys Leadership Transition: Understanding Personality Types

In the late 1990s, Infosys was emerging as one of India's leading IT companies. The company was co-founded by N. R. Narayana Murthy, who was widely respected for his vision, leadership, and values. As Infosys grew, it became clear that the company needed a new leadership structure to manage its expanding operations and global presence.

This transition phase became a critical test for Infosys, highlighting the importance of understanding and managing different personality types within its leadership team.

The Challenge of Leadership Transition

As Infosys expanded, it was evident that the leadership team would need to evolve. N. R. Narayana Murthy, known for his analytical and calm approach, was considering stepping back from day-to-day operations to make way for new leadership. The company had several highly capable leaders, each with their distinct personalities and management styles. However, the differences in these personalities soon became a point of contention.

For example, Nandan Nilekani, who would later succeed Murthy as CEO, was known for his energetic and dynamic approach. He was a visionary, much like Murthy, but with a more aggressive style of leadership. In contrast, S. Gopalakrishnan (Kris), another co-founder, was known for his methodical and calm demeanor, preferring a more consensus-driven approach.

As Infosys prepared for its leadership transition, these personality differences began to surface. The challenge was not only in choosing the right leader but also in ensuring that the leadership team could work effectively together despite their varying approaches to decision-making and problem-solving.

Managing the Transition

Recognizing the potential for conflict, Murthy and the board took steps to manage the transition carefully. They organized several workshops and retreats where the leadership team could discuss their management styles, expectations, and concerns. These sessions were designed to help the leaders understand each other's personalities better and to align with the company's vision and strategy.

Murthy also emphasized the importance of maintaining Infosys' core values, regardless of who was at the helm. He believed that a shared commitment to these values would help bridge the differences in personalities and ensure a smooth transition.

One of the key moments in this process was when Murthy openly discussed his own personality and leadership style with the team. He shared how his calm and reflective approach had shaped the company's culture and encouraged others to reflect on how their personalities influenced their leadership styles. This transparency had set the tone for honest and open communication within the team.

The Outcome

The leadership transition at Infosys was ultimately successful, with Nandan Nilekani taking over as CEO in 2002. The process highlighted the importance of understanding personality types within a leadership team and the need for open communication to manage these differences effectively. Nilekani's dynamic leadership helped Infosys continue its growth trajectory, while Gopalakrishnan's methodical approach ensured that the company remained grounded in its values.

Infosys' ability to navigate this transition was a testament to the strength of its leadership team and their understanding of each other's personalities. The company's success during this period underscores the importance of recognizing and managing different personality types in any team, particularly at the leadership level.

The Infosys leadership transition is a powerful example of how understanding personality types can play a critical role in the success of a team. By acknowledging and addressing the differences in their leadership styles, Infosys was able to ensure a smooth transition and continue its growth as one of India's leading IT companies. This story serves as a reminder that effective teamwork often requires not only recognizing but also embracing the diverse personalities within a team.

1.2.3 Leveraging Strengths and Mitigating Weaknesses

Understanding individual differences isn't just about managing conflicts—it's also about leveraging each team member's strengths and mitigating their weaknesses. A great leader knows how to bring out the best in each person, ensuring that the team's collective strengths are greater than the sum of its parts.

The Story of Sundar Pichai and the Chrome Browser Team

Sundar Pichai, the CEO of Alphabet Inc. and Google, is renowned for his ability to leverage individual strengths and mitigate weaknesses within his teams. A notable example of his leadership style can be seen in his role in the development and success of the Google Chrome browser. This story highlights how Pichai effectively understood and utilized the diverse strengths of his team members, turning their collective potential into a groundbreaking product.

The Challenge of Developing Google Chrome

In 2008, Google was ready to venture into the web browser market, a space dominated by Internet Explorer and Firefox. Sundar Pichai, who was then a Vice President of Product Management at Google, was tasked with leading the development of Google Chrome. The project was ambitious, aiming to create a faster, more secure, and user-friendly browser.

Pichai faced a significant challenge: building a team with the right mix of skills and expertise to execute this vision. The team included a variety of specialists, each with their strengths and weaknesses. For instance, some engineers who excelled in performance optimization, others who were experts in user interface design, and some who had deep knowledge in security protocols.

Leveraging Strengths

Pichai's approach to managing the Chrome team was to first identify each member's core strengths and then align their responsibilities accordingly. He understood that the success of the Chrome project would depend on utilizing the unique skills of each team member effectively.

Performance Optimization Experts: Pichai assigned engineers with a strong background in performance optimization to focus on making Chrome faster than its competitors. Their expertise in improving speed and efficiency was crucial in ensuring that the browser would meet users' expectations for quick load times.

User Interface Designers: Engineers with a flair for design were tasked with creating an intuitive and visually appealing user interface. Pichai recognized the importance of a sleek, user-friendly design in differentiating Chrome from existing browsers.

Security Specialists: Given the importance of security in web browsing, Pichai leveraged the knowledge of team members who specialized in security to build robust defenses against potential threats. Their role was critical in ensuring that Chrome would be a safe option for users.

Pichai encouraged collaboration among these specialists, fostering an environment where their individual strengths could complement each other. He facilitated regular meetings where team members could share their progress, challenges, and insights. This approach ensured that the team remained aligned and that each member's expertise contributed to the project's overall success.

Mitigating Weaknesses

While leveraging strengths was a key strategy, Pichai also focused on addressing and mitigating the weaknesses of the team. Recognizing that no team is without its flaws, he took several steps to ensure that these weaknesses did not hinder the project:

- Skill Gaps: To address any skill gaps, Pichai arranged for additional training and brought in external consultants when needed. For example, if a team member was struggling with a particular technical challenge, Pichai ensured they had access to the necessary resources or expertise to overcome it.

- Communication Barriers: Pichai was aware that different team members might have varying communication styles, which could lead to misunderstandings. To mitigate this, he established clear communication protocols and encouraged open dialogue among team members. This helped in addressing any issues early and maintaining a cohesive team dynamic.
- Workload Management: To prevent burnout and ensure productivity, Pichai was attentive to the workload of each team member. He monitored progress and adjusted responsibilities as needed, ensuring that no one was overwhelmed and that the team remained balanced.

The Outcome

Under Sundar Pichai's leadership, the first beta version of Google Chrome was launched in September 2008 and quickly became a major success. The browser was praised for its speed, simplicity, and security features. Chrome's rapid growth in market share can be attributed to the effective use of the team's strengths and the successful management of their weaknesses.

Pichai's ability to leverage individual strengths while addressing weaknesses played a crucial role in the project's success. His leadership ensured that each team member's unique skills contributed to the development of a product that exceeded user expectations.

The development of Google Chrome under Sundar Pichai's leadership is a powerful example of how understanding and leveraging individual strengths, while mitigating weaknesses, can lead to exceptional outcomes.

Pichai's approach to team management not only resulted in a highly successful product but also demonstrated the importance of aligning team members' strengths with project goals. This story serves as a valuable lesson for leaders on the significance of recognizing and harnessing the diverse capabilities within their teams.

The Role of Leadership in Team Dynamics

Leadership plays a crucial role in shaping team dynamics. A good leader sets the tone for how the team interacts, makes decisions, and handles challenges. In this section, we'll explore how different leadership styles impact team dynamics and provide real-world examples of leadership in action.

1.3.1 Leadership Styles and Their Impact

Different leadership styles can have a profound impact on team dynamics. Some leaders take a directive approach, making decisions and giving clear instructions, while others take a more participative approach, involving the team in decision-making.

The Directive Leader vs. The Participative Leader

In a large healthcare organization, two department heads were known for their contrasting leadership styles. The first, Dr. Singh, was a directive leader. He made decisions quickly and expected his team to follow his instructions without question. His approach was efficient, but it often left team members feeling disengaged and undervalued.

The second department head, Dr. Patel, was a participative leader. She involved her team in decision-making, encouraging open discussions and valuing input from all team members. While this approach sometimes took more time, it fostered a sense of ownership and collaboration within the team.

When both departments were faced with a major challenge—a sudden increase in patient admissions due to a flu outbreak—the differences in their leadership styles became evident. Dr. Singh's team struggled to adapt to the increased workload, with team members feeling overwhelmed and disconnected. In contrast, Dr. Patel's team worked together seamlessly, coming up with innovative solutions to manage the increased demand.

The outcome was clear: Dr. Patel's participative leadership style had created a strong, cohesive team that was able to navigate the crisis effectively. Dr. Singh's directive style, while efficient in stable times, had failed to build the resilience needed to handle a crisis.

This story highlights the impact of different leadership styles on team dynamics. While there is no one-size-fits-all approach to leadership, understanding how your leadership style influences your team is key to building a successful, dynamic team.

1.3.2 The Role of Emotional Intelligence

In addition to leadership style, emotional intelligence (EI) plays a critical role in how leaders influence team dynamics. Leaders with high emotional intelligence are able to understand and manage their own emotions, as well as the emotions of their team members.

The Transformation of Ratan Tata at Tata Group

Ratan Tata, the former Chairman of Tata Group, is celebrated for his exceptional emotional intelligence (EI) and its profound impact on one of India's largest and most respected conglomerates. Tata's leadership journey exemplifies how emotional intelligence—encompassing empathy, self-awareness, and the ability to manage emotions—can significantly influence an organization's culture and performance. This story illustrates how Tata's EI played a pivotal role in transforming the Tata Group during a period of significant change.

The Challenge at Tata Group

When Ratan Tata took over as Chairman of Tata Group in 1991, the conglomerate was facing a complex set of challenges. The Indian economy was transitioning from a controlled to a liberalized market, creating both opportunities and uncertainties for businesses. Tata Group needed to adapt to this new environment, manage a diverse portfolio of companies and navigate the global expansion of its operations.

One of Tata's primary challenges was to modernize Tata Group while preserving its traditional values and fostering a culture of integrity and social responsibility. Tata's approach to these challenges was deeply influenced by his emotional intelligence, which guided him in steering the organization through these turbulent times.

Empathy and Human Connection

Tata's empathy and ability to connect with people were central to his leadership style:

- Understanding Employees' Concerns: Tata was known for his genuine concern for the well-being of employees. During his tenure, he prioritized employee welfare, especially during challenging times. For example, during the economic downturn in the early 2000s, Tata made a point to avoid layoffs and instead worked to find ways to support and retain employees. His empathy helped maintain morale and loyalty among the workforce.
- Support During Crisis: In the aftermath of the 2008 Mumbai attacks, Tata demonstrated remarkable empathy and support. The Tata Group's Taj Mahal Palace Hotel was one of the primary sites attacked. Tata personally visited the site and expressed his solidarity with the employees who had suffered and the families who had lost loved ones. His presence and supportive actions were instrumental in helping the organization recover and rebuild.

Self-Awareness and Vision

Tata's self-awareness was crucial in guiding Tata Group through a period of transformation:

- Acknowledging and Adapting to Change: Tata was aware of the need for Tata Group to adapt to the changing business landscape. He embraced the shift from a focus solely on traditional industries to a more diversified approach. This included expanding into technology and global markets. Tata's self-awareness allowed him to recognize when changes were necessary and to lead the organization through these transitions effectively.

- Balancing Tradition and Modernity: Tata understood the importance of preserving Tata Group's core values while embracing modernization. He championed initiatives that aligned with the company's ethical standards and social responsibility while also pursuing innovative business strategies. This balance helped maintain the company's reputation while driving growth.

Managing Emotions and Conflict

Tata's ability to manage emotions and resolve conflicts was evident in several key situations:

- Navigating Internal Disputes: Tata adeptly handled internal conflicts within the conglomerate, especially when integrating newly acquired companies. For instance, during the acquisition of Corus Group, Tata managed the integration process with sensitivity to the concerns of both the acquired and acquiring teams. His approach to conflict resolution emphasized communication and mutual respect, which facilitated smoother transitions.
- Handling External Challenges: Tata also faced external challenges with emotional intelligence. When Tata Motors launched the Nano, the world's cheapest car, it faced significant criticism and challenges related to production and marketing. Tata managed these issues with a calm and measured approach, focusing on addressing concerns and finding solutions rather than

reacting defensively.

The Impact of Tata's Leadership

Ratan Tata's emotional intelligence had a lasting impact on the Tata Group:

- Cultural Transformation: Tata successfully modernized Tata Group while upholding its traditional values of integrity, social responsibility, and excellence. His leadership fostered a culture of mutual respect and empathy, which contributed to high employee engagement and loyalty.
- Global Expansion and Innovation: Under Tata's leadership, Tata Group expanded its global footprint and diversified its portfolio. The acquisitions of Corus, Jaguar Land Rover, and the launch of the Nano are testament to the company's successful adaptation to the global market. Tata's emotional intelligence played a crucial role in navigating these complex endeavors.
- Ratan Tata's leadership of Tata Group exemplifies the profound impact of emotional intelligence on organizational success. His empathy, self-awareness and ability to manage emotions and conflicts helped transform Tata Group during a period of significant change. Tata's story demonstrates how high emotional intelligence can drive positive cultural and operational outcomes, making him a notable example for leaders seeking to harness the power of EI in their own organizations.

1.3.3 Leading Through Conflict

Conflict is an inevitable part of any team's dynamics. How leaders handle conflict can either strengthen or weaken the team. Effective leaders understand that conflict, when managed well, can lead to growth and innovation.

The Story of Dr. Reddy's Laboratories and G.V. Prasad

Dr. Reddy's Laboratories, a prominent Indian pharmaceutical company, faced a significant internal conflict during the early 2000s. The company was transitioning from a domestic-focused business model to an international one, which created substantial friction within the organization. G.V. Prasad, co-chairman and CEO of Dr. Reddy's Laboratories, played a crucial role in managing and resolving these conflicts, showcasing effective leadership in a time of considerable organizational change.

The Conflict: Global Expansion vs. Domestic Operations

Dr. Reddy's Laboratories had established itself as a leading pharmaceutical company in India. However, as the company sought to expand its footprint globally, it encountered resistance from within. The shift towards international markets meant a change in strategic focus, operational adjustments and cultural realignment, which caused friction among employees and executives who were accustomed to the company's domestic-centric approach.

Managing the Conflict

Navigating Organizational Change:

- Communication and Vision: Prasad recognized that clear communication was essential to managing this conflict. He organized town hall meetings and strategic workshops where he outlined the vision for international expansion. By articulating the long-term benefits of global diversification and how it aligned with the company's growth strategy, Prasad was able to address concerns and build a shared sense of purpose.
- Inclusive Leadership: To manage resistance, Prasad adopted an inclusive approach. He involved key leaders and stakeholders in discussions about the international strategy. By valuing their input and addressing their concerns, he reduced opposition and fostered a collaborative environment. This inclusivity helped in aligning different factions within the company with the new strategic direction.

Handling Cultural and Operational Adjustments:

- Cultural Integration: As Dr. Reddy's expanded into new markets, integrating diverse cultures became a significant challenge. Prasad understood the importance of cultural sensitivity and implemented cross-cultural training programs. These programs were designed to help employees understand and navigate the cultural nuances of the international markets they were entering.

- Operational Realignment: The operational shifts required for global expansion also created friction. Prasad worked closely with operational teams to streamline processes and address any logistical issues. He facilitated workshops and training sessions to equip employees with the skills needed for the new operational requirements, thus easing the transition and reducing conflicts.

Resolution and Outcomes

G.V. Prasad's approach to managing conflict during Dr. Reddy's Laboratories' global expansion proved to be effective. By fostering open communication, involving key stakeholders and addressing both cultural and operational challenges, he was able to lead the company through a successful transformation. Dr. Reddy's Laboratories not only expanded its global presence but also established itself as a prominent player in the international pharmaceutical market.

The story of Dr. Reddy's Laboratories and G.V. Prasad highlights the critical role of effective conflict management in leading organizational change. Prasad's leadership demonstrated that addressing internal conflicts with transparency, inclusivity and a focus on cultural and operational integration can turn challenges into opportunities for growth and success. This approach underscores the importance of skilled conflict management in strengthening teams and driving organizational achievements.

Building a High-Performing Team

Understanding team dynamics is the first step in building a high-performing team. In this section, we'll explore practical strategies for fostering trust, communication, collaboration and effective leadership within your team.

1.4.1 Fostering Trust and Psychological Safety

As we've seen, trust and psychological safety are the foundation of any successful team. Building trust requires consistent, transparent communication, as well as a commitment to creating an environment where team members feel safe to express themselves.

Strategies for Fostering Trust:

- Lead by Example: As a leader, demonstrate trustworthiness through your actions. Be consistent, keep your promises and show respect for all team members.
- Encourage Open Communication: Create channels for open and honest communication. Encourage team members to share their thoughts, ideas, and concerns without fear of judgment.
- Acknowledge Mistakes: When mistakes happen, address them openly and constructively. Encourage a culture of learning from mistakes rather than placing blame.
- Celebrate Successes Together: Recognize and celebrate team achievements, both big and small. This helps build

a sense of shared success and reinforces the value of each team member's contributions.

1.4.2 Enhancing Communication

Effective communication is essential for aligning the team's efforts and ensuring that everyone is working towards the same goal. It's important to establish clear communication channels and set expectations for how information is shared.

Strategies for Enhancing Communication:

- Regular Check-Ins: Hold regular team meetings to keep everyone informed and aligned. Use these meetings to discuss progress, address challenges and share updates.
- Clear and Concise Messaging: When communicating important information, be clear and concise. Avoid jargon or ambiguity and make sure that everyone understands the message.
- Active Listening: Encourage active listening within the team. When someone is speaking, ensure that others are fully engaged and focused on understanding their perspective.
- Feedback Loops: Establish feedback loops to ensure that communication is a two-way street. Encourage team members to provide feedback on processes, decisions, and communication styles.

1.4.3 Encouraging Collaboration

Collaboration is the key to unlocking the full potential of your team. To foster collaboration, create an environment where team members feel empowered to share ideas, work together and contribute to the team's success.

Strategies for Encouraging Collaboration:

- Cross-Functional Teams: Consider forming cross-functional teams for specific projects. This allows team members with different skills and perspectives to work together, leading to more innovative solutions.
- Collaborative Tools: Use collaborative tools and platforms to facilitate teamwork. Whether it's a project management tool, a shared document platform, or a communication app, having the right tools in place can enhance collaboration.
- Shared Goals: Ensure that the team has a clear understanding of the shared goals and objectives. When everyone is working towards the same goal, collaboration becomes more natural.
- Team Building Activities: While crisis situations can be powerful for team bonding, regular team-building activities can also play a role in strengthening collaboration. These activities should focus on building trust, improving communication and fostering a sense of unity.

1.4.4 Developing Effective Leadership

Effective leadership is essential for guiding the team and shaping its dynamics. Leaders must be able to adapt their style to the needs of the team and the challenges they face.

Strategies for Developing Effective Leadership:

- Self-Awareness: As a leader, develop self-awareness of your strengths, weaknesses, and leadership style. Understand how your approach impacts the team and be willing to adapt as needed.
- Emotional Intelligence: Cultivate emotional intelligence by being attuned to the emotions and needs of your team members. Use this awareness to create a supportive and empathetic work environment.
- Conflict Resolution Skills: Develop conflict resolution skills to handle disagreements and conflicts within the team. Encourage constructive debates and facilitate solutions that benefit the team as a whole.
- Continuous Learning: Leadership is a continuous learning process. Seek out opportunities for professional development, whether through training, mentoring, or self-study. The more you learn, the better equipped you'll be to lead your team effectively.

Conclusion

Understanding team dynamics is crucial for any leader who wants to build a high-performing team. By fostering trust, enhancing communication, encouraging collaboration and developing effective leadership, you can create a team that not only meets its goals but thrives in the face of challenges.

In the next chapters, we'll explore how to apply these principles in the context of crisis situations, turning challenges into opportunities for team bonding and success. By understanding and mastering team dynamics, you'll be better equipped to lead your team through any challenge that comes your way.

CHAPTER TWO

The Myth of Team Building Activities

In the corporate world, team-building activities have become a ubiquitous tool for managers and leaders looking to foster camaraderie and collaboration within their teams. From weekend retreats and trust falls to escape rooms and cooking classes, companies invest significant time and resources into these activities with the hope of creating strong, cohesive teams. But do these activities really work? Or are they just superficial gestures that fail to address the deeper issues within a team?

This chapter explores the myth of team-building activities, challenging the conventional wisdom that they are the key to building strong teams. Through real-world examples and stories, we will examine why these activities often fall short and what truly drives team bonding.

The Rise of Team Building Activities

Team-building activities have their roots in the early 20th century when companies began to recognize the importance of employee morale and collaboration. The idea was simple: bring employees together outside of their regular work environment to engage in fun, non-work-related activities, thereby fostering a sense of unity and teamwork.

Over time, team-building activities evolved into a wide array of events, ranging from simple icebreakers and trust exercises to elaborate retreats and adventure-based challenges. The underlying assumption was that by participating in these activities, team members would develop stronger relationships, leading to improved communication, collaboration and productivity back at the office.

The Fortune 500 Company's Annual Retreat

Consider the example of a Fortune 500 company that, like many others, organizes an annual team-building retreat for its employees. Every year, the company takes its staff to a luxury resort for a weekend filled with activities such as zip-lining, team sports, and cooking competitions. The goal is to give employees a break from their daily routines and create opportunities for them to bond in a relaxed, informal setting.

On the surface, the retreat seems like a success. Employees have fun, engage in friendly competition, and get to know their colleagues outside of work. However, when they return to the office, the effects of the retreat are often short-lived. The same issues that existed before—such as communication breakdowns, lack of trust and siloed working—quickly resurface.

This story is not unique. Many companies invest heavily in team-building activities, yet they struggle to see long-term improvements in team dynamics and performance. This raises the question: Are these activities truly effective, or are they merely a band-aid solution?

The Limits of Superficial Bonding

One of the main criticisms of traditional team-building activities is that they often focus on creating superficial bonds rather than addressing the deeper issues within a team. While it's true that these activities can be enjoyable and may temporarily boost morale, they rarely lead to lasting change.

2.2.1 The Problem with Forced Fun

One of the most common complaints about team-building activities is that they can feel forced or artificial. Employees are often required to participate in activities that they may not enjoy or find meaningful, leading to feelings of resentment or disengagement.

The Reluctant Participant at a Sales Team's Outing

Consider the story of Ramesh, an introverted sales team member at a mid-sized company. The team was scheduled to participate in a day-long team-building event at an escape room, an activity chosen by the team leader to promote problem-solving and collaboration under pressure. While the leader believed that the event would bring the team closer together, the psychological impact on Ramesh was quite the opposite.

Understanding Ramesh's Psychological Experience

Ramesh is introverted, a personality trait characterized by a preference for solitary or low-stimulation environments. Introverts often find group activities, especially those involving competition or time pressure, overwhelming. For Ramesh, the escape room scenario—where quick thinking, teamwork, and constant interaction were required—triggered feelings of anxiety and stress. This discomfort was compounded by the social anxiety he experienced, which is common in individuals who fear judgment or negative evaluation in social settings.

During the event, Ramesh's discomfort was visible to his colleagues, yet the group dynamic did not allow for an open discussion about his unease. Psychological safety, a term coined by Harvard professor Amy Edmondson, refers to a team environment where individuals feel safe to express their thoughts, concerns and vulnerabilities without fear of negative consequences. In Ramesh's case, the lack of psychological safety meant that he couldn't voice his discomfort or opt out of the activity without feeling judged.

Instead of fostering a sense of belonging, the escape room experience left Ramesh feeling more isolated and disconnected from his team. His inability to fully engage with the activity due to his psychological discomfort led to frustration, both for him and his teammates. This frustration can be understood through the lens of cognitive dissonance—the mental discomfort experienced when one's behaviour conflicts with their beliefs or values. Ramesh valued collaboration but felt unable to contribute meaningfully in a high-pressure, competitive environment.

Ramesh's experience is not unique. Many employees face similar challenges when participating in team-building activities that do not align with their personality, preferences or psychological needs. The forced nature of these activities can lead to resentment, disengagement and even a deterioration of team relationships. In Ramesh's case, what was intended to be a bonding experience instead created division, highlighting the potential pitfalls of one-size-fits-all approaches to team building.

2.2.2 The Temporary Nature of Team-Building "Highs"

Even when team-building activities are enjoyable and well-received, their positive effects are often short-lived. The excitement and camaraderie generated during the activity can quickly fade once employees return to their regular work routines.

The Short-Lived Impact of a Corporate Retreat

A large financial services company organizes a weekend retreat in the mountains for its leadership team. The retreat includes outdoor activities, team challenges, and motivational speakers. The team returns to the office on Monday feeling energized and connected, with a renewed sense of purpose and collaboration.

However, within a few weeks, the pressures of work begin to erode the positive effects of the retreat. Deadlines, conflicts and the demands of daily operations take precedence, and the team gradually reverts to its previous patterns of communication and collaboration. The bonds that were formed during the retreat weaken, and the retreat's impact on team dynamics diminishes.

This story highlights a common issue with team-building activities: they often create a temporary "high" that doesn't translate into lasting change. While these activities can be a fun break from the routine, they rarely address the underlying issues that affect team performance.

Why Traditional Team Building Falls Short

To understand why traditional team-building activities often fail to achieve their intended outcomes, it's important to examine the underlying assumptions and limitations of these activities.

2.3.1 The Fallacy of the One-Size-Fits-All Approach

Many team-building activities are based on a one-size-fits-all approach, assuming that what works for one team will work for another. However, teams are made up of individuals with diverse personalities, preferences, and working styles. What resonates with one group may not resonate with another.

The Misguided Team-Building Workshop

A technology company decides to hold a team-building workshop for its engineering department. The workshop is designed to improve communication and collaboration, with activities such as role-playing exercises and group discussions. However, the engineers are a highly analytical and introverted group, and they find the activities awkward and uncomfortable.

Instead of fostering communication, the workshop creates a sense of discomfort and disengagement. The engineers feel that the activities are not relevant to their work and that the workshop is a waste of time. As a result, the workshop fails to achieve its goals, and the team dynamics remain unchanged.

This story illustrates the limitations of a one-size-fits-all approach to team building. Teams are unique, and what works for one team may not work for another. To be effective, team-building activities need to be tailored to the specific needs and characteristics of the team.

2.3.2 The Disconnect Between Team Building and Work

Another limitation of traditional team-building activities is the disconnect between the activities themselves and the actual work that the team does. While activities like trust falls or cooking classes can be fun, they often have little relevance to the team's day-to-day tasks and challenges.

The Trust Fall That Didn't Translate to Trust at Work

A marketing agency holds a team-building day that includes a series of trust-building exercises, including the classic trust fall. The team members enjoy the day and have fun participating in the activities. However, when they return to the office, they find that the trust fall exercise didn't translate to increased trust in the workplace.

The team continues to struggle with issues of communication and collaboration, and the trust-building day has little impact on their ability to work together effectively. The disconnect between the team-building activities and the team's actual work means that the day was largely a missed opportunity.

This story highlights the importance of aligning team-building activities with the team's work. For team building to be effective, it needs to be relevant to the challenges and tasks that the team faces on a daily basis.

2.3.3 The Illusion of Quick Fixes

Traditional team-building activities are often seen as a quick fix for deeper issues within a team. However, team dynamics are complex and cannot be easily resolved with a single event or activity.

The CEO's Misguided Attempt to Fix a Dysfunctional Team

A CEO at a manufacturing company is concerned about the dysfunction within one of the company's key teams. The team has been struggling with communication breakdowns, missed deadlines and interpersonal conflicts. In an effort to address these issues, the CEO decides to organize a team-building day at a local adventure park.

The team enjoys the day and participates enthusiastically in the activities. However, when they return to the office, the underlying issues that caused the dysfunction remain unresolved. The adventure day, while fun, did little to address the root causes of the team's problems.

The CEO's attempt to use a team-building activity as a quick fix ultimately fails because it doesn't address the deeper issues within the team. True team building requires a more thoughtful and sustained approach, one that goes beyond superficial activities and tackles the underlying dynamics at play.

The True Drivers of Team Bonding

If traditional team-building activities often fall short, what does truly drive team bonding? The answer lies in the real-world challenges and experiences that teams face together. When teams are put in situations that require them to work together to overcome obstacles, solve problems, and achieve common goals, they naturally develop stronger bonds.

2.4.1 The Power of Shared Challenges

One of the most powerful drivers of team bonding is the experience of facing shared challenges. When a team is confronted with a difficult task or crisis, they are forced to rely on each other, communicate effectively, and work together to find solutions.

The Story of Amul's Success

The power of shared challenges in team dynamics cannot be overstated. When a team confronts a difficult task or crisis, they are compelled to rely on each other, communicate effectively, and work collaboratively to find solutions. One of the most compelling examples of this phenomenon comes from India's dairy industry, where a collective struggle against exploitation led to the creation of one of the country's most successful cooperative societies: Amul.

In the early 1940s, the dairy farmers in the Kaira district of Gujarat, India, faced severe exploitation from middlemen and the British-controlled Polson Dairy, which had a monopoly on the local dairy industry. These middlemen would purchase milk from farmers at extremely low prices, leaving the farmers with barely enough to cover their costs. The farmers had no bargaining power and were trapped in a cycle of poverty.

The situation was dire, and the farmers were growing increasingly desperate. It was in this context that Tribhuvandas Kishibhai Patel, a local farmer leader, and Sardar Vallabhbhai Patel, India's future first Deputy Prime Minister, recognized the need for a collective approach to counter this exploitation. They understood that only by coming together and pooling their resources could the farmers hope to break free from the oppressive system.

The Power of Collective Action

In 1946, under the guidance of Sardar Vallabhbhai Patel and the technical expertise of Dr. Verghese Kurien, the farmers decided to form a cooperative society that would buy and market their milk directly. This cooperative was named the Kaira District Co-operative Milk Producers' Union, which later became known as Amul, derived from the Sanskrit word "Amulya," meaning priceless or invaluable.

The formation of the cooperative was not without its challenges. The farmers had little experience in running a business, let alone a large-scale dairy operation. They faced resistance from entrenched interests, including Polson

Dairy, which attempted to undermine their efforts. However, the farmers were united by a shared goal: to gain control over the prices of their milk and improve their livelihoods.

Shared Challenges and Team Bonding

The initial years were tough. The cooperative had to build its infrastructure from scratch, including establishing milk collection centers, creating a cold chain system, and finding reliable buyers for their milk. The farmers had to contribute their milk to the cooperative even when the prices were uncertain, trusting that their collective efforts would pay off in the long run.

This shared challenge of building a cooperative from the ground up created a strong sense of unity among the farmers. They were no longer competing against each other; instead, they were working together to achieve a common goal. The trust they placed in each other and in their leaders was crucial in overcoming the numerous obstacles they faced.

The Psychological Impact of Shared Challenges

From a psychological perspective, the Amul story illustrates the concept of collective efficacy, which refers to a group's shared belief in its ability to achieve a common goal. The farmers' collective struggle against exploitation and their joint efforts to build a successful cooperative strengthened their sense of community and mutual support. This collective efficacy was a key factor in Amul's success.

Moreover, the experience of facing and overcoming shared challenges enhanced the farmers' resilience, the ability to bounce back from adversity. The process of building Amul required them to adapt to new roles, learn new skills, and persevere through difficult times. This resilience not only helped them in their business endeavors but also improved their self-confidence and sense of agency.

Amul's Success and Legacy

The collective efforts of the farmers, guided by visionary leaders like Dr. Verghese Kurien, eventually paid off. Amul grew from a small cooperative into a massive success, transforming the lives of millions of dairy farmers across India. Today, Amul is one of the largest dairy brands in the world, known for its high-quality products and innovative marketing strategies.

The success of Amul is a testament to the power of shared challenges in building strong, cohesive teams. The farmers who founded Amul were not just working together to sell milk; they were united by a common struggle against exploitation and a shared vision for a better future. This sense of purpose and collective effort was the foundation of their success.

The story of Amul is a powerful example of how shared challenges can bring a team together and lead to remarkable achievements. When a group of individuals is united by a common goal and faces adversity together, they can build strong bonds, develop collective efficacy, and achieve outcomes that would be impossible to attain individually. The experience of overcoming challenges as a team not only strengthens the group but also empowers each member, fostering a sense of pride and accomplishment that can drive future success.

Amul's journey from a small cooperative to a global dairy giant is a reminder that the most effective teams are often forged in the crucible of shared challenges. By working together to overcome obstacles, teams can build the trust, resilience, and collective strength needed to achieve their goals and make a lasting impact.

2.4.2 The Importance of Purpose and Meaning

Another key driver of team bonding is a shared sense of purpose and meaning. When team members are united by a common goal or mission, they are more likely to develop strong, lasting bonds.

The Story of Aravind Eye Care System

A shared sense of purpose can elevate a team from merely working together to creating something extraordinary. When a team is driven by a common mission that resonates deeply with each member, the bonds formed are not just professional but personal. This sense of purpose and meaning can lead to unparalleled dedication and commitment. A prime example of this is the story of Aravind Eye Care System in India.

The Visionary Leadership of Dr. Govindappa Venkataswamy

Aravind Eye Care System was founded in 1976 by Dr. Govindappa Venkataswamy, affectionately known as Dr. V. After retiring from government service, where he had performed thousands of cataract surgeries, Dr. V had a vision to eradicate needless blindness in India. This was no small feat, given the scale of the problem in India at the time, where millions suffered from preventable blindness due to cataracts and other treatable eye conditions.

Dr. V started Aravind with just 11 beds in a small hospital in Madurai, Tamil Nadu. The initial team was small but deeply committed to the cause. Dr. V's vision was not just about treating patients; it was about creating a sustainable model that could provide high-quality eye care to everyone, regardless of their ability to pay. The team was united by this mission of serving the poor and restoring sight to the blind, which gave their work a profound sense of meaning.

The Power of Purpose

The team at Aravind Eye Care was driven by a shared belief that they were part of something much bigger than themselves. This belief in the purpose of their work led to extraordinary levels of dedication. For example, many of the doctors and nurses would work long hours without complaint, driven by the knowledge that their efforts could transform lives. The sense of purpose was so strong that many employees viewed their work as a calling rather than just a job.

The psychological concept of intrinsic motivation was at play here. The staff at Aravind Eye Care were not driven primarily by external rewards like salary or recognition; instead, they were motivated by the internal satisfaction of contributing to a noble cause. This intrinsic motivation led to high levels of engagement, resilience, and a strong sense of community within the team.

Growth and Success Through Shared Meaning

Under Dr. V's leadership, Aravind Eye Care grew exponentially. The small hospital in Madurai expanded to become a network of hospitals, clinics, and outreach programs across India. Despite this growth, the core mission remained unchanged: to eliminate needless blindness. The team's shared sense of purpose continued to bind them together, even as the organization expanded.

Dr. V's vision also extended to creating a model that could be replicated worldwide. The Aravind model became a subject of study and emulation globally, and the organization began training doctors and healthcare professionals from other countries. The success of Aravind Eye Care is a testament to the power of a shared mission in creating a cohesive and effective team.

The story of Aravind Eye Care System illustrates how a shared sense of purpose and meaning can drive a team to achieve extraordinary results. When team members are united by a common goal that resonates deeply with them, they are more likely to overcome challenges, work collaboratively, and stay committed to the cause. The bonds formed through such a shared mission are strong and enduring, providing the foundation for sustained success. Dr. V's legacy at Aravind Eye Care is a powerful example of how purpose-driven teams can change the world.

2.4.3 The Role of Leadership in Facilitating Team Bonding

While shared challenges and a sense of purpose are powerful drivers of team bonding, effective leadership is also essential. Leaders play a critical role in creating the conditions for team bonding to occur.

The Story of Captain Rakesh Sharma

Effective leadership is crucial in shaping the dynamics of a team. While challenges and a shared sense of purpose can bring a team together, it is often the leader who creates the environment in which these factors can flourish. A leader's vision, actions, and attitude toward their team can significantly influence how well team members bond with each other. The story of Captain Rakesh Sharma, India's first astronaut, illustrates how leadership can play a pivotal role in facilitating team bonding, especially under challenging circumstances.

Captain Rakesh Sharma and the Soyuz T-11 Mission

Captain Rakesh Sharma was an Indian Air Force pilot who became the first Indian to travel in space when he flew aboard the Soviet spacecraft Soyuz T-11 in 1984. The mission was a collaborative effort between the Indian Space Research Organisation (ISRO) and the Soviet space program. Sharma was accompanied by two Soviet cosmonauts, Commander Yuri Malyshev and Flight Engineer Gennadi Strekalov. Although Sharma was highly skilled, he was stepping into an entirely new environment, with different cultural dynamics and a language barrier to navigate.

The Leadership of Commander Yuri Malyshev

Commander Yuri Malyshev was the leader of the Soyuz T-11 mission. Understanding the unique challenges posed by such an international collaboration, Malyshev took a proactive approach to ensure that the team bonded well before embarking on the mission. He knew that the success of the mission would depend not only on their technical skills but also on how well the team could work together under the stressful and confined conditions of space travel.

Malyshev's leadership style was inclusive and empathetic. He made it a point to learn about Indian culture, even picking up a few Hindi phrases to communicate better with Sharma. This gesture might seem small, but it had a profound psychological impact, as it helped bridge the cultural gap and made Sharma feel more at ease.

Understanding the psychological concept of social cohesion, Malyshev organized several informal gatherings and discussions during their training period. These sessions were not just about technical briefings but also about getting to know each other on a personal level. Malyshev encouraged open communication, where team members could express their concerns and ideas freely. This approach helped in building trust and mutual respect among the team members.

Building Trust and Camaraderie

During their training, there were moments of tension and uncertainty, as the crew had to master complex procedures and simulate emergency scenarios. Malyshev's leadership was instrumental in maintaining morale during these times. He knew that fear and anxiety could undermine team cohesion, so he fostered an environment where team members felt supported. He would often take time to talk individually with Sharma and Strekalov, ensuring that they were mentally prepared for the mission.

Malyshev also understood the importance of collective efficacy, a psychological concept where a group's shared belief in its ability to achieve goals plays a crucial role in its performance. He consistently emphasized the team's collective strengths rather than individual weaknesses. This focus on the team as a whole rather than on individual roles helped in building a strong sense of unity.

The Mission and Its Success

When the Soyuz T-11 mission finally launched on April 3, 1984, the crew was a well-bonded unit. Their shared training experiences, underpinned by Malyshev's effective leadership, ensured that they operated seamlessly as a team. In space, the crew conducted various experiments, including Earth observation and materials testing, with precision and coordination.

One of the most memorable moments of the mission was when Captain Rakesh Sharma, during a live telecast, was asked by then-Prime Minister Indira Gandhi how India looked from space. His now-famous reply, "Saare Jahan Se Achha" (Better than the entire world), reflected not just national pride but also the strong emotional bond he had formed with his Soviet counterparts, who had come to understand and respect his culture and background through their leader's efforts.

The Soyuz T-11 mission was a success, and much of its success can be attributed to the leadership of Commander Yuri Malyshev, who skillfully facilitated the bonding of a culturally diverse team. His efforts ensured that the team not only achieved its objectives but also returned as a unified group, with each member having deep respect and admiration for the others.

The story of Captain Rakesh Sharma and the Soyuz T-11 mission demonstrates the critical role of leadership in facilitating team bonding. Effective leaders, like Commander Yuri Malyshev, understood the importance of creating an environment where team members could connect on a personal level, trust each other, and work together towards a common goal. By focusing on building social cohesion and collective efficacy, leaders can turn diverse groups into tightly-knit teams capable of achieving great things, even in the most challenging circumstances.

Rethinking Team Building: Strategies for Success

If traditional team-building activities are not the answer, what are the alternatives? In this section, we'll explore strategies for building strong teams that go beyond superficial activities and address the deeper dynamics within a team.

2.5.1 Creating Opportunities for Shared Experiences

One of the most effective ways to build strong teams is to create opportunities for shared experiences that are relevant to the team's work. These experiences should challenge the team, require collaboration, and align with the team's goals and purpose.

Strategy: Engaging in Real-World Challenges

Instead of organizing artificial team-building activities, consider engaging your team in real-world challenges that require them to work together. This could be a complex project, a difficult problem to solve, or a crisis that needs to be managed. These experiences will create natural opportunities for team bonding.

Example: The Cross-Functional Project That Built a Strong Team

A technology company assigns a cross-functional team to work on a new product development project. The project is challenging and requires collaboration between engineers, designers, marketers, and salespeople. As the team works together to overcome obstacles and achieve milestones, they develop a strong sense of trust and camaraderie. The shared experience of working towards a common goal creates bonds that last long even after the project is completed.

2.5.2 Fostering a Culture of Trust and Psychological Safety

Building a strong team requires more than just shared experiences; it also requires a culture of trust and psychological safety. Team members need to feel safe to express themselves, share their ideas, and take risks without fear of judgment or reprisal.

Strategy: Encouraging Open Communication

Encourage open communication within your team by creating an environment where team members feel comfortable to speak . This includes actively listening to team members, valuing their input, and addressing concerns in a constructive manner.

Example: The Manager Who Built Trust Through Open Communication

A manager at a financial service company recognizes that her team is struggling with communication issues. To address this, she implements regular team meetings where team members are encouraged to share their thoughts, ideas, and concerns. She also holds one-on-one meetings to provide individual support and feedback. Over time, the team begins to communicate more openly, leading to stronger relationships and better collaboration.

2.5.3 Aligning Team Building with the Team's Purpose

For team building to be effective, it needs to be aligned with the team's purpose and goals. Activities and experiences should be relevant to the team's work and contribute to the achievement of the team's objectives.

Strategy: Integrating Team Building into the Work

Rather than separating team building from the team's work, integrate it into the work itself. This means creating opportunities for team members to collaborate, solve problems, and achieve goals together as part of their daily tasks.

Example: The Agile Team That Built Bonds Through Collaboration

An agile software development team uses sprints and regular retrospectives as opportunities for team building. By working together to plan, execute, and review their work, the team members develop strong bonds and a sense of shared purpose. The collaborative nature of their work fosters trust and camaraderie, leading to a high-performing team.

2.5.4 Embracing Continuous Learning and Improvement

Building a strong team is an ongoing process that requires continuous learning and improvement. Teams should regularly reflect on their dynamics, identify areas for growth, and take steps to improve their collaboration and performance.

Strategy: Facilitating Regular Team Reflection

Encourage your team to engage in regular reflection and feedback. This could involve holding retrospectives, conducting team assessments, or simply having open discussions about what's working and what's not. Use these reflections as opportunities to learn and grow as a team.

Example: The Team That Grew Stronger Through Continuous Improvement

A project management team at a construction company conducts regular retrospectives at the end of each project phase. During these sessions, the team reflects on their performance, identifies areas for improvement, and sets goals for the next phase. This process of continuous reflection and improvement helps the team build stronger relationships and achieve better results over time.

Conclusion: Moving Beyond the Myth

The myth of traditional team-building activities is pervasive in the corporate world, but it's time to move beyond it. While these activities can be fun and may temporarily boost morale, they are often superficial and fail to address the deeper dynamics within a team.

True team bonding is not achieved through artificial activities, but through shared challenges, a sense of purpose, and effective leadership. By creating opportunities for real-world experiences, fostering a culture of trust, aligning team-building with the team's purpose, and embracing continuous improvement, leaders can build strong, cohesive teams that are capable of achieving great things.

As we continue in this book, we will explore how to apply these principles in the context of crisis situations, turning challenges into opportunities for team bonding and success. By understanding and mastering the true drivers of team bonding, you will be better equipped to lead your team through any challenge that comes your way.

Crisis as a Catalyst

In the world of business, crises are often seen as something to be avoided at all costs. They bring uncertainty, stress, and the potential for failure. But what if, instead of viewing crises as threats, we began to see them as opportunities—opportunities to bring people together, to forge stronger teams, and to achieve great things?

In this chapter, we'll explore the concept of crisis as a catalyst for team bonding and growth. Through real-life examples and stories, we'll examine how crises can be used as powerful tools for building strong, cohesive teams. We'll also look at the role of leadership in navigating crises and turning them into opportunities for success.

The Nature of Crisis

Before we dive into the specifics of how crises can be catalysts for team bonding, it's important to understand what we mean by "crisis." A crisis is any event or situation that disrupts the normal functioning of an organization or team. This disruption can take many forms, from a sudden loss of a key client to a major technical failure or even a global pandemic.

Crises are characterized by their unpredictability and the sense of urgency they create. They often require quick decision-making, adaptability, and collaboration. While crises can be incredibly challenging, they also have the potential to bring out the best in people and teams.

3.1.1 The Dual Nature of Crisis: Threat and Opportunity

Crisis, by its very nature, is a double-edged sword. On one side, it presents a threat—something that can lead to failure, loss, or harm. On the other side it presents an opportunity—a chance to rise to the occasion, to innovate, and to grow stronger as a team.

Threat and Opportunity: Kiran Mazumdar-Shaw and the Crisis at Biocon

Crises are often perceived as negative events—unwelcome disruptions that pose significant threats to organizations, teams, and individuals. However, crises also carry the potential to be catalysts for change, innovation, and growth. This dual nature of crises—where threat and opportunity coexist—is vividly illustrated in the true story of Kiran Mazumdar-Shaw, the founder of Biocon, one of India's leading biotechnology companies.

Kiran Mazumdar-Shaw is a pioneering entrepreneur in India's biotech industry. When she started Biocon in 1978, she faced numerous challenges, including skepticism about a woman leading a business in a male-dominated field, the fledgling nature of the biotech industry in India, and limited financial resources. However, the most significant crisis that tested her and her company came in the early

2000s.

The Threat: A Sudden Regulatory Clampdown

In the early 2000s, Biocon had established itself as a leader in the production of enzymes for the food and beverage industry. The company was thriving, and its future looked promising. However, in 2001, the company faced a severe crisis when the Indian government imposed a sudden regulatory clampdown on the import of raw materials essential for enzyme production. The new regulations threatened to disrupt Biocon's supply chain, halting production and jeopardizing the company's reputation and financial stability.

For Kiran Mazumdar-Shaw, this crisis posed an existential threat to Biocon. The company's entire business model was at risk, and the livelihoods of hundreds of employees were in jeopardy. The crisis tested her leadership, resilience, and ability to navigate through uncertainty.

The Opportunity: Pivoting to Biopharmaceuticals

Rather than succumbing to the threat, Kiran Mazumdar-Shaw saw the crisis as an opportunity to pivot and diversify Biocon's business. She recognized that relying solely on enzyme production made the company vulnerable to external factors like regulatory changes. With her vision and determination, she decided to steer Biocon into the biopharmaceutical industry, a field that was still in its nascent stages in India but held immense potential.

The transition was not easy. It required significant investment in research and development, acquiring new expertise, and building state-of-the-art manufacturing facilities. Mazumdar-Shaw also faced resistance from within her team, as many were apprehensive about venturing into an uncharted territory. However, she believed that this crisis was an opportunity to innovate and secure Biocon's future.

Overcoming the Crisis: Innovation and Growth

Under Mazumdar-Shaw's leadership, Biocon developed its first biopharmaceutical product, recombinant human insulin, which was a significant achievement not only for the company but for India's healthcare industry. The product was launched in India at an affordable price, making life-saving insulin accessible to millions of diabetic patients who could not afford imported brands.

This bold move into biopharmaceuticals paid off. Biocon grew from being an enzyme producer to becoming a global biopharmaceutical company. The crisis that initially threatened the company's existence ultimately propelled it into a new phase of growth and innovation.

Character Revealed: Resilience and Vision

Kiran Mazumdar-Shaw's response to the crisis revealed her remarkable resilience and visionary leadership. She did not see the regulatory clampdown as merely a threat but as a signal that Biocon needed to evolve. Her ability to turn a potentially devastating situation into an opportunity for innovation exemplifies the psychological concept of cognitive reframing—the practice of changing the way one perceives a situation to see the positive possibilities.

Moreover, her actions demonstrated transformational leadership. She inspired her team to embrace change, guided them through uncertainty, and aligned them with a new vision. This crisis also highlighted her risk-taking propensity, a characteristic often associated with successful entrepreneurs, which involves the willingness to take bold actions in the face of uncertainty.

The Dual Nature of Crisis

The story of Kiran Mazumdar-Shaw and Biocon underscores the dual nature of crisis. While crises undoubtedly pose significant threats, they also present opportunities for those who are willing to see them as such. In this case, what could have been a catastrophic event for Biocon became the turning point that transformed the company into a global leader in biopharmaceuticals.

Kiran Mazumdar-Shaw's ability to navigate the crisis with resilience, innovation, and vision turned the threat into an opportunity for growth and success. Her story serves as a powerful reminder that in every crisis, there lies the potential for transformation—if we are willing to see beyond the immediate threat and seize the opportunities that emerge.

Crises test the true character of leaders and organizations. They challenge us to confront our vulnerabilities but also offer us the chance to innovate, grow, and emerge stronger. The dual nature of crisis—where threat and opportunity coexist—requires leaders who can see beyond the immediate danger and guide their teams toward a future filled with possibility. Kiran Mazumdar-Shaw's journey through the crisis at

Biocon is a testament to the power of seeing opportunity in adversity and leading with vision and resilience.

3.1.2 The Power of a Common Goal

In a crisis, the entire team is united by a common goal: to overcome the challenge and emerge successful. This shared purpose can be a powerful force, aligning everyone's efforts and creating a sense of unity.

The Power of a Common Goal: The Staff of Taj Mahal Palace Hotel During the 26/11 Mumbai Attacks

When a team faces a crisis, the presence of a common goal can become the guiding light that unites everyone and drives collective efforts toward overcoming the challenge. This story of the 2008 Taj Mahal Palace Hotel attack in Mumbai, India, demonstrates how a shared purpose can empower a team to rise above fear and uncertainty.

On November 26, 2008, a series of terrorist attacks shook Mumbai to its core. Among the targets was the iconic Taj Mahal Palace Hotel, a symbol of India's hospitality and heritage. As gunmen stormed the hotel, chaos erupted, and the lives of hundreds of guests and staff members were thrown into grave danger.

In the midst of this terrifying crisis, the staff of the Taj Mahal Palace Hotel, led by General Manager Karambir Kang, displayed extraordinary courage and dedication. Despite the immense personal risk, the staff members made a collective decision to prioritize the safety of their guests above their own lives. They were driven by a singular common goal: to protect and save as many lives as possible.

The hotel staff, from chefs and waiters to security personnel, worked together seamlessly. They led guests to safe areas, provided them with food and water, and comforted those who were in shock. Many staff members even formed human shields to protect guests from the attackers. Their actions were not the result of any formal crisis training but stemmed from a deep sense of duty and a shared commitment to the safety and well-being of their guests.

One of the most poignant examples of this shared purpose was the story of Taj chef Hemant Oberoi, who led a group of guests through the hotel's narrow service corridors to safety. Despite the danger, he made multiple trips back into the hotel to rescue others, driven by the belief that he could not leave anyone behind. His leadership and courage were instrumental in saving many lives that night.

General Manager Karambir Kang himself lost his wife and children, who were trapped in a room on the sixth floor of the hotel. Despite this personal tragedy, Kang continued to coordinate rescue operations and support his staff, never wavering from the common goal of protecting the guests.

When the siege finally ended after nearly 60 hours, the bravery and selflessness of the Taj Mahal Palace Hotel staff had saved hundreds of lives. Their actions became a symbol of resilience and humanity in the face of terror.

The story of the Taj Mahal Palace Hotel staff during the 26/11 Mumbai attacks is a powerful example of how a common goal can unite a team, even in the most harrowing circumstances. Their shared commitment to guest safety allowed them to transcend fear and personal loss, ultimately transforming a crisis into a testament to the strength and solidarity of the human spirit. This story underscores the profound impact that a common goal can have on team dynamics, particularly in times of crisis.

3.1.3 Crisis as a Test of Character

Crises often bring out the true character of individuals and teams. When faced with adversity, people reveal their strengths, weaknesses, and values. This process can be transformative, both for individuals and for the team as a whole.

The Story of Arun and the Chennai Floods

In December 2015, Chennai, one of India's largest cities, was hit by devastating floods. The relentless rainfall over several weeks led to a crisis of unprecedented magnitude. Homes were submerged, power was cut off, and thousands of people were stranded without basic necessities. It was a time when the true character of individuals and teams was tested.

Arun Krishnamurthy, the founder of the Environmentalist Foundation of India (EFI), was one such individual whose character shone through during this crisis. Mr. Arun had always been passionate about environmental conservation, and EFI was known for its work in cleaning lakes and raising environmental awareness. However, the floods brought a different kind of challenge—one that required quick thinking, leadership, and above all, a deep sense of empathy.

As the floodwaters rose, Mr. Arun could have focused solely on ensuring the safety of his own family and friends. But instead, he saw the crisis as a call to action. Recognizing the gravity of the situation, Mr. Arun mobilized a team of volunteers from EFI and beyond. Together, they braved the floodwaters to rescue stranded residents, distribute food and water, and provide medical assistance to those in need.

What made Mr. Arun's efforts stand out was not just the physical aid he provided, but the way he led his team through the crisis. Mr. Arun's calm demeanor and clear sense of purpose inspired those around him. He was decisive yet compassionate, ensuring that every decision was made with the well-being of others in mind. When resources were scarce, Mr. Arun prioritized the most vulnerable—children, the elderly, and those with medical conditions.

Throughout the crisis, Mr. Arun's character was revealed in the way he handled adversity. He showed resilience in the face of overwhelming odds, courage in situations that would have paralyzed many, and an unwavering commitment to his values. But it wasn't just Mr. Arun's character that was tested and revealed; the crisis also brought out the best in his team.

Under Mr. Arun's leadership, the volunteers displayed incredible teamwork and solidarity. They worked tirelessly, often in dangerous conditions, without seeking recognition or reward. The crisis had brought them closer together, forging bonds that would last long after the floodwaters receded. The experience was transformative for the team, as they saw firsthand the impact of their efforts and the importance of staying true to their values, even in the most challenging circumstances.

Mr. Arun Krishnamurthy's actions during the Chennai floods are a powerful reminder of how crises can test and reveal character. In times of adversity, true leaders like Mr. Arun emerge, demonstrating that character is not just about words or intentions, but about actions taken when it matters most. This story also illustrates how crises can transform teams, bringing individuals together in a shared mission and leaving them stronger and more united in the end.

The Role of Leadership in a Crisis

While crises can naturally bring teams together, the role of leadership is critical in turning a crisis into a catalyst for bonding and growth. Effective leaders can guide their teams through difficult times, ensuring that the crisis strengthens rather than weakens the team.

3.2.1 Leading with Vision and Clarity

In a crisis, uncertainty is one of the biggest challenges. Team members may feel anxious, confused, or overwhelmed. A leader's ability to provide vision and clarity is crucial in helping the team navigate through the crisis.

Leading with Vision and Clarity: N. Chandrasekaran's Leadership During the 2008 Financial Crisis

In times of crisis, uncertainty can paralyze even the most experienced teams. When the future is unclear and the stakes are high, a leader's ability to provide a clear vision and direction can be the difference between success and failure. The story of how N. Chandrasekaran, the then-CEO of Tata Consultancy Services (TCS), led his team through the 2008 global financial crisis, illustrates the power of leading with vision and clarity.

In 2008, the global financial crisis sent shockwaves across industries, and the IT sector was no exception. Tata Consultancy Services (TCS), one of India's largest IT services companies, was particularly vulnerable due to its reliance on international markets, especially in the United States and Europe. As clients tightened their budgets and cut back on IT spending, TCS faced the prospect of declining revenues and shrinking margins.

The crisis created a sense of fear and uncertainty among employees. Many were concerned about job security, the company's future, and how they would navigate the turbulent economic environment. It was in this challenging context that N. Chandrasekaran, who had recently taken over as CEO, had to steer the company through the storm.

Recognizing the need for a clear and decisive response, Chandrasekaran quickly articulated a vision that would not only address the immediate challenges but also position TCS for long-term success. He understood that in order to maintain morale and keep the team focused, it was essential to communicate this vision clearly and consistently.

Clarity in Communication

One of Chandrasekaran's first steps was to address the company's employees directly. In a series of town hall meetings and internal communications, he acknowledged the gravity of the situation but also emphasized TCS's inherent strengths, such as its diverse portfolio, deep client relationships, and robust delivery model. He reassured employees that while the road ahead would be tough, TCS had the resilience and capability to emerge stronger.

Chandrasekaran's message was clear: TCS would not simply weather the storm, but would use the crisis as an opportunity to innovate, optimize operations, and strengthen client partnerships. He laid out a three-pronged strategy focused on cost optimization, enhancing operational efficiency, and deepening client engagement.

Vision for the Future

Beyond the immediate crisis management, Chandrasekaran also articulated a vision for the future. He saw the financial crisis as a catalyst for change in the IT services industry and believed that TCS could lead this transformation. He envisioned a future where TCS would not only be a service provider but a strategic partner to its clients, helping them navigate their own challenges through technology and innovation.

To achieve this, Chandrasekaran encouraged the development of new service offerings and solutions that would be relevant in a post-crisis world. He pushed for investments in emerging technologies like cloud computing, data analytics, and digital services, anticipating that these would be the growth drivers of the future. This forward-looking approach helped TCS differentiate itself from competitors who were more focused on short-term survival.

Empowering the Team

Chandrasekaran also understood that leading with vision and clarity required empowering his team to execute on the strategy. He ensured that senior leaders across the organization were aligned with the vision and had the autonomy to make decisions that would drive the company forward. This approach fostered a sense of ownership and accountability among leaders and managers, which in turn inspired confidence among employees.

Under Chandrasekaran's leadership, TCS not only navigated the financial crisis successfully but also emerged as a stronger and more competitive company. The company's revenues continued to grow, and it solidified its position as a global leader in IT services. Chandrasekaran's ability to provide vision and clarity during a time of profound uncertainty was instrumental in this success.

The story of N. Chandrasekaran's leadership during the 2008 financial crisis is a testament to the importance of vision and clarity in times of uncertainty. By providing a clear and compelling vision, communicating it effectively, and empowering his team to execute on it, Chandrasekaran was able to guide TCS through one of the most challenging periods in its history. This story highlights how effective leadership can transform a crisis into an opportunity for growth and innovation.

3.2.2 Empowering the Team to Take Ownership

Another critical aspect of leadership during a crisis is empowering the team to take ownership of the situation. When team members feel that they have a stake in the outcome, they are more likely to be engaged, motivated, and collaborative.

Empowering the Team to Take Ownership: Sanjiv Mehta and the Transformation of Hindustan Unilever

Empowering a team to take ownership during a crisis is critical for driving engagement and achieving successful outcomes. When team members feel they have a stake in the outcome, their motivation and collaboration increase, leading to better results. A notable example of this principle in action is the story of how Sanjiv Mehta, CEO of Hindustan Unilever Limited (HUL), navigated the company through a challenging period of transformation and growth.

In 2013, Sanjiv Mehta took over as CEO of Hindustan Unilever Limited (HUL), one of India's largest consumer goods companies. HUL was facing significant challenges, including declining growth in key markets and a need to rejuvenate its brand portfolio to remain competitive. The company also needed to adapt to changing consumer preferences and market dynamics.

Mehta recognized that addressing these challenges required more than just a strategic overhaul; it required empowering his team to take ownership of the transformation process. Here's how he approached this task:

Empowering the Team

Building a Shared Vision: Mehta started by communicating a clear and compelling vision for HUL's future. He articulated a strategy focused on innovation, sustainable growth, and market leadership. By sharing this vision, he helped the team understand the broader goals and how their individual contributions were vital to achieving them.

Encouraging Ownership and Initiative: To foster a sense of ownership, Mehta encouraged employees at all levels to take initiative and contribute ideas. He implemented a program called "Project Shakti," which aimed to empower rural women to become micro-entrepreneurs selling HUL products in their communities. This initiative not only created new business opportunities but also gave team members a direct stake in the company's success.

Fostering Collaboration and Accountability: Mehta promoted a culture of collaboration by breaking down silos within the organization. He established cross-functional teams to work on key projects and encouraged open communication and collaboration between departments. By doing so, he ensured that team members felt accountable for their contributions and understood their role in the larger context.

Providing Support and Resources: Understanding the importance of support in driving ownership, Mehta ensured that his team had access to the resources and tools needed to succeed. He invested in training and development programs to enhance employees' skills and capabilities, and he provided necessary financial and logistical support for new initiatives.

Under Sanjiv Mehta's leadership, Hindustan Unilever successfully navigated its transformation and achieved significant growth. The company revitalized its brand portfolio, introduced innovative products, and expanded its market presence. The success of "Project Shakti" exemplified the power of empowering team members, as it created a new business model that contributed to both social impact and revenue growth.

The sense of ownership fostered by Mehta's leadership not only drove successful outcomes but also strengthened the company's culture. Employees felt more engaged and motivated, leading to higher levels of performance and collaboration.

Sanjiv Mehta's approach to empowering his team during Hindustan Unilever's transformation is a compelling example of effective leadership in a crisis. By building a shared vision, encouraging ownership and initiative, fostering collaboration, and providing support, Mehta enabled his team to take ownership of the company's challenges. This empowerment not only led to successful outcomes but also strengthened the team's commitment and engagement. The story highlights the critical role of empowering teams during crises to achieve long-term success and drive organizational growth.

Turning Crisis into Opportunity: Strategies for Leaders

While crises are inherently challenging, they also present unique opportunities for leaders to strengthen their teams. In this section, we'll explore practical strategies for turning crisis into opportunity, drawing on the lessons and examples we've discussed.

3.3.1 Embrace the Crisis Mindset

One of the most important strategies for turning crisis into opportunity is to embrace the crisis mindset. This means viewing crises not as threats to be avoided, but as opportunities for growth, innovation, and bonding.

Strategy: Reframe the Crisis

As a leader, you can help your team reframe the crisis by focusing on the potential positive outcomes. Emphasize the opportunities for learning, innovation, and collaboration that the crisis presents. Encourage your team to see the crisis as a challenge to be met, rather than a disaster to be feared.

Example: The Startup That Thrived During a Market Downturn

A technology startup faced a significant crisis when the market for its product suddenly contracted. The company's future was in jeopardy, and the team was feeling demoralized. The CEO, however, saw an opportunity to innovate. He challenged the team to pivot the product to meet new market demands, and he empowered them to explore creative solutions.

The team embraced the challenge, and through intense collaboration and experimentation, they developed a new version of the product that quickly gained traction in the market. The crisis not only saved the company but also brought the team closer together and reinforced their sense of purpose.

This example demonstrates the power of reframing a crisis as an opportunity. By embracing the crisis mindset, leaders can inspire their teams to innovate and grow in the face of adversity.

3.3.2 Foster a Culture of Resilience

Resilience is the ability to bounce back from adversity and continue moving forward. In a crisis, resilience is essential for both individuals and teams. Leaders can play a key role in fostering a culture of resilience within their teams.

Strategy: Build Psychological Safety

Psychological safety is the foundation of resilience. When team members feel safe to express their ideas, take risks, and make mistakes without fear of judgment or retribution, they are more likely to be resilient in the face of crisis.

As a leader, you can build psychological safety by encouraging open communication, valuing diverse perspectives, and supporting team members through challenges. When team members know that they have each other's backs, they are more likely to be resilient and to come together in a crisis.

Example: The Pharmaceutical Company's Response to a Product Recall

A pharmaceutical company faced a major crisis when one of its flagship products was found to have a manufacturing defect that required a nationwide recall. The company's leadership knew that the crisis could damage their reputation and financial standing, but they also saw it as an opportunity to demonstrate their commitment to quality and patient safety.

The company's leadership fostered a culture of resilience by encouraging open communication and collaboration across departments. Teams were empowered to take ownership of the recall process, from identifying affected products to communicating with healthcare providers and patients. The company's transparent and proactive response not only mitigated the crisis but also strengthened its relationships with stakeholders.

The crisis brought the company's teams closer together, as they worked collaboratively to address the challenges. The experience reinforced the importance of psychological safety and resilience in navigating crises.

This example highlights the role of psychological safety in fostering resilience during a crisis. By creating an environment where team members feel supported and valued, leaders can help their teams navigate adversity and emerge stronger.

3.3.3 Encourage Innovation and Adaptability

Crises often require teams to think outside the box and come up with creative solutions to unprecedented challenges. Leaders can encourage innovation and adaptability by creating an environment where experimentation and learning are valued.

Strategy: Promote a Growth Mindset

A growth mindset is the belief that abilities and intelligence can be developed through dedication and hard work. In a crisis, a growth mindset can help teams embrace challenges, learn from mistakes, and continuously improve.

As a leader, you can promote a growth mindset by encouraging your team to view challenges as opportunities for growth. Celebrate successes and learn from failures, and create an environment where innovation is rewarded.

Example: The Automotive Company's Response to a Supply Chain Disruption

An automotive company faced a significant crisis when a key supplier went out of business, disrupting the supply chain for a critical component. The company's production was at risk, and the leadership knew that they needed to find a solution quickly.

The company's leadership encouraged the engineering and procurement teams to innovate and explore alternative solutions. The teams experimented with different suppliers, materials, and production methods, ultimately developing a new approach that not only resolved the crisis but also improved the product's performance.

The experience fostered a culture of innovation and adaptability within the company. The teams learned to embrace challenges as opportunities for growth and to continuously seek out new ways to improve.

This example illustrates how encouraging innovation and adaptability can help teams navigate crises and turn them into opportunities for improvement.

Conclusion: Crisis as a Catalyst for Transformation

As we've explored in this chapter, crises are powerful catalysts for team bonding and growth. While they are inherently challenging, they also present unique opportunities for teams to come together, innovate, and achieve great things.

By understanding the dual nature of crisis—as both a threat and an opportunity—leaders can help their teams navigate adversity and turn it into a source of strength.

Through vision, clarity, empowerment, and resilience, leaders can transform crises into opportunities for bonding and success.

As we continue in this book, we will delve deeper into specific strategies for leading teams through crises, using real-life examples and lessons from history. By mastering the art of crisis management, you will be better equipped to lead your team through any challenge and turn adversity into a catalyst for transformation.

CHAPTER FOUR

The Role of Leadership During a Crisis

In times of crisis, the role of leadership is not just important—it is crucial. Leaders are the guiding force that can determine whether a team succumbs to the pressure or rises above it. When a crisis hits, people naturally look to their leaders for direction, reassurance, and strength. This chapter explores the multifaceted role of leadership during a crisis, highlighting the qualities, actions, and decisions that can transform a potential disaster into an opportunity for growth and cohesion.

Through detailed analysis and real-world examples, this chapter will demonstrate how effective leadership can turn a crisis into a defining moment for a team and organization. We will delve into the key leadership qualities needed in a crisis, examine the importance of communication, discuss how to inspire and motivate teams under pressure, and explore the balance between decisiveness and empathy. By the end of this chapter, you will have a clear understanding of how to lead effectively during a crisis and how to leverage such situations to strengthen your team.

The Qualities of Effective Leadership in a Crisis

The effectiveness of a leader during a crisis largely depends on their qualities and how they manifest in times of pressure. While different situations may require different approaches, certain core qualities are universally important.

4.1.1 Courage and Resilience

Courage and resilience are perhaps the most critical qualities a leader can possess during a crisis. Courage allows leaders to face the unknown, make difficult decisions, and take responsibility for the outcome, no matter how uncertain. Resilience, on the other hand, enables leaders to remain steadfast and focused, even when the situation seems dire.

Story: Winston Churchill During World War II

One of the most iconic examples of courageous and resilient leadership is Winston Churchill during World War II. When Churchill became Prime Minister of the United Kingdom in 1940, the country was facing its darkest hours. Nazi Germany had conquered much of Europe, and Britain was next in line.

Churchill's leadership during this crisis was defined by his unwavering courage and resilience. Despite the overwhelming odds, he refused to consider defeat. His famous speeches, filled with defiance and determination, inspired the British people to stand firm and resist the enemy. Churchill's resilience in the face of adversity was instrumental in keeping the nation's morale high, ultimately contributing to the eventual victory.

Churchill's leadership during World War II is a testament to the power of courage and resilience. These qualities not only helped him lead his country through a crisis but also solidified his legacy as one of history's greatest leaders.

4.1.2 Decisiveness and Adaptability

In a crisis, the ability to make quick, decisive decisions is crucial. However, leaders must also be adaptable, as the situation can change rapidly. The best leaders are those who can balance decisiveness with flexibility, making decisions based on the best available information while remaining open to new data and changing circumstances.

Story: The Apollo 13 Crisis

The Apollo 13 mission, as discussed in the previous chapter, is a prime example of how decisiveness and adaptability can be critical in a crisis. When an oxygen tank exploded two days into the mission, NASA's leadership was faced with a life-or-death situation. The initial plan was no longer viable, and the team had to quickly adapt to the new reality.

NASA's Flight Director, Gene Kranz, played a pivotal role in the crisis. His decisive leadership and adaptability were crucial in guiding the team through the crisis. Kranz made quick decisions about shutting down non-essential systems to conserve power, reconfiguring the spacecraft's trajectory, and developing a new plan to bring the astronauts home safely. His ability to remain calm, decisive, and adaptable in the face of unprecedented challenges was instrumental in the successful resolution of the crisis.

Kranz's leadership during the Apollo 13 crisis illustrates the importance of decisiveness and adaptability in a crisis. Leaders should be able to make quick decisions while remaining flexible enough to adapt to changing circumstances.

4.1.3 Empathy and Emotional Intelligence

While decisiveness and resilience are critical, they must be balanced with empathy and emotional intelligence. A crisis can be an incredibly stressful time for a team, and leaders who understand and address the emotional needs of their team members can foster a sense of trust and unity.

Story: Jacinda Ardern and the Christchurch Attack

In March 2019, New Zealand experienced one of its darkest days when a gunman attacked two mosques in Christchurch, killing 51 people. The country was in shock, and the situation required not just decisive leadership but also deep empathy.

New Zealand's Prime Minister, Jacinda Ardern, demonstrated remarkable empathy and emotional intelligence in the wake of the attack. She immediately reached out to the Muslim community, offering her condolences and support. Ardern's decision to wear a hijab while meeting with survivors and victims' families was a powerful gesture of solidarity and empathy. Her actions not only provided comfort to those affected but also helped unify the country in the face of tragedy.

Ardern's leadership during the Christchurch attack is a powerful example of how empathy and emotional intelligence are crucial during a crisis. By addressing the emotional needs of her people, she was able to foster a sense of unity and resilience in the face of a devastating tragedy.

The Importance of Communication During a Crisis

Communication is the lifeblood of effective crisis management. In times of uncertainty, clear, consistent, and transparent communication can make all the difference. It helps to manage expectations, reduce anxiety, and ensure that everyone is on the same page.

4.2.1 Transparency and Honesty

During a crisis, people crave transparency and honesty from their leaders. Sugarcoating the situation or withholding information can lead to mistrust and confusion. Leaders who communicate openly and honestly, even when the news is bad, are more likely to earn the trust and respect of their teams.

Story: The Samsung Galaxy Note 7 Crisis

In 2016, Samsung faced one of the most significant crises in its history. The launch of the Galaxy Note 7, a flagship smartphone, quickly turned into a nightmare when reports emerged that the device's batteries were prone to overheating and catching fire. What was supposed to be a market-leading product soon became a symbol of failure, leading to a global recall that cost the company billions of dollars and severely damaged its reputation.

The crisis was exacerbated by initial missteps in communication. When the first reports of overheating devices surfaced, there was confusion within Samsung about the severity of the problem. The company's initial response was to issue a small-scale recall and replacement program, which only compounded the issue when the replacement devices also began to catch fire. The lack of clear, transparent communication both internally and externally worsened the situation.

Recognizing the gravity of the crisis, Samsung's leadership, led by CEO Kwon Oh-hyun, took decisive action to change course. They realized that the only way to regain trust—both within the company and among consumers—was to foster open communication at all levels.

Internally, Samsung created an environment where employees were encouraged to speak openly about the issues they were encountering. Engineers, designers, and quality assurance teams were brought together in cross-functional meetings to discuss the root causes of the battery failures. Leadership made it clear that there would be no finger-pointing; the focus was on finding a solution rather than assigning blame. This shift in communication culture allowed employees to express their concerns and ideas without fear, leading to a more thorough investigation of the problem.

Externally, Samsung adopted a policy of transparency with its customers, regulators, and the media. The company issued public apologies and provided regular updates on the progress of the recall and the ongoing investigation into the causes of the fire. Samsung even took the unprecedented step of releasing the full findings of their internal investigation, showing that the battery issues were due to both design flaws and manufacturing errors. This level of openness was risky, but it was crucial in rebuilding trust.

Samsung's commitment to open communication during the crisis extended beyond the immediate response. In the months following the recall, the company implemented new safety measures, including an eight-point battery safety check, and launched a global marketing campaign to reassure customers that the issues had been resolved. Samsung's leadership made a point of communicating these changes not just through traditional media but also by engaging directly with customers through social media, forums, and live Q&A sessions.

The crisis surrounding the Galaxy Note 7 was a defining moment for Samsung. While the financial impact was severe, the company's decision to foster open communication during the crisis helped it to recover and rebuild its reputation. By encouraging transparency, listening to employees, and being honest with the public, Samsung was able to turn a disastrous situation into an opportunity for learning and improvement. The experience reinforced the importance of clear communication in times of crisis—a lesson that has since become deeply ingrained in Samsung's corporate culture.

4.2.2 Consistency and Clarity

In a crisis, inconsistent or unclear communication can lead to confusion and panic. Leaders must ensure that their messages are consistent across all channels and that they are clear about what is happening, what is being done, and what is expected from everyone involved.

Story: The BP Oil Spill

In 2010, BP faced a massive crisis when the Deepwater Horizon oil rig exploded, leading to one of the worst environmental disasters in history. The company's response to the crisis was widely criticized, and one of the key issues was its communication.

BP's communication during the crisis was often inconsistent and unclear. For example, the company initially downplayed the scale of the spill, which led to public outrage when the true extent of the disaster became apparent.

Additionally, BP's CEO, Tony Hayward, made several public statements that were seen as tone-deaf and dismissive of the situation, further damaging the company's reputation.

The BP oil spill crisis is a cautionary tale about the importance of consistency and clarity in crisis communication. Leaders must ensure that their messages are consistent, clear, and sensitive to the situation at hand to avoid further exacerbating the crisis.

Inspiring and Motivating Teams Under Pressure

A crisis can be a demoralizing and stressful experience for a team. Effective leaders know how to inspire and motivate their teams, even in the most challenging circumstances. By fostering a sense of purpose, providing support, and recognizing the team's efforts, leaders can help their teams stay focused and committed.

4.3.1 Creating a Sense of Purpose

One of the most powerful motivators in a crisis is a clear sense of purpose. When team members understand the importance of their work and how it contributes to overcoming the crisis, they are more likely to stay engaged and motivated.

Story: The Miracle on the Hudson

In January 2009, US Airways Flight 1549 struck a flock of geese shortly after takeoff, causing both engines to fail. The plane's captain, Chesley "Sully" Sullenberger, made the decision to land the plane on the Hudson River in New York City. All 155 passengers and crew members survived, and the event became known as the "Miracle on the Hudson."

Sullenberger's leadership during the crisis was marked by a clear sense of purpose. He remained calm and focused, understanding that his primary responsibility was to save the lives of everyone on board. His clear sense of purpose guided his decisions and actions, ultimately leading to a successful outcome.

The Miracle on the Hudson is an example of how a clear sense of purpose can guide leadership during a crisis. When leaders focus on the mission at hand and communicate that purpose to their teams, they can inspire and motivate their teams to achieve extraordinary results.

4.3.2 Providing Support and Encouragement

In a crisis, leaders must provide not only direction but also emotional support to their teams. Recognizing the stress and anxiety that team members may be feeling, and offering encouragement and support, can help to keep morale high.

Story: The Rescue of the Wild Boars Soccer Team

In June 2018, 12 boys and their soccer coach were trapped in a flooded cave in Thailand. The rescue operation, which lasted 17 days, was one of the most complex and dangerous in history. The situation was dire, and the team's survival depended on the efforts of a large international group of divers, military personnel, and volunteers.

Throughout the rescue operation, the leadership of the Thai Navy SEALs and the international diving team was critical. The leaders provided not only technical expertise but also emotional support to their teams. They recognized the immense pressure that everyone was under and made it a priority to offer encouragement and reassurance.

The successful rescue of the Wild Boars soccer team is a testament to the importance of providing support and encouragement in a crisis. Leaders who recognize the emotional needs of their teams and offer support can help to maintain morale and focus, even in the most challenging situations.

Balancing Decisiveness with Empathy

In a crisis, leaders are often required to make difficult decisions quickly. However, it is essential to balance decisiveness with empathy. Making decisions without considering the human impact can lead to resentment and a loss of trust. Conversely, being overly empathetic without making necessary decisions can result in inaction and further complications.

4.4.1 The Importance of Compassionate Leadership

Compassionate leadership involves understanding and addressing the emotional and psychological needs of team members while still making the tough decisions necessary to navigate the crisis. It's about finding the balance between being firm and being understanding.

Story: Arne Sorenson and Marriott's Response to the COVID-19 Pandemic

The COVID-19 pandemic had a devastating impact on the global hospitality industry, and Marriott International was no exception. The company faced massive losses as travel ground to a halt, and difficult decisions had to be made regarding layoffs and furloughs.

Marriott's CEO, Arne Sorenson, became known for his compassionate leadership during this crisis. In a video message to employees, Sorenson spoke candidly about the challenges the company was facing and the difficult decisions that were being made. He expressed deep empathy for the employees who were affected and committed to doing everything possible to support them during the crisis.

Sorenson's approach to leadership during the pandemic was a model of balancing decisiveness with empathy. He made the tough decisions needed to keep the company afloat while also showing compassion and understanding for those impacted by the crisis. His leadership helped to maintain employee trust and loyalty during an incredibly challenging time.

Decision-Making Under Pressure

Decision-making during a crisis is often a test of a leader's abilities. The pressure to make the right decision quickly can be overwhelming, especially when the stakes are high. However, effective leaders use a combination of intuition, experience, and data to make informed decisions under pressure.

4.5.1 Leveraging Experience and Expertise

In a crisis, leaders often have to rely on their experience and expertise to make decisions quickly. However, they must also be open to input from others who may have different perspectives or specialized knowledge.

Story: Ernest Shackleton and the Endurance Expedition

In 1914, explorer Ernest Shackleton set out on the Endurance expedition to Antarctica. The goal was to cross the continent, but the expedition quickly turned into a survival mission when the ship became trapped in ice and was eventually crushed.

Shackleton's leadership during the crisis is legendary. He made the decision to abandon the original mission and focus solely on the survival of his crew. His experience and knowledge of the polar environment guided his decisions, but he also relied heavily on the expertise of his crew members. Shackleton's ability to make quick, informed decisions, while also valuing the input of his team, was crucial in ensuring that all 28 crew members survived the ordeal.

Shackleton's leadership during the Endurance expedition is a powerful example of decision-making under pressure. His ability to leverage his experience and the expertise of his team members was key to their survival.

4.5.2 The Role of Intuition in Crisis Decision-Making

While data and experience are important, intuition also plays a critical role in decision-making during a crisis. Leaders often have to make decisions with incomplete information, and their intuition can help guide them in the right direction.

Story: The Cuban Missile Crisis

In 1962, the world came to the brink of nuclear war during the Cuban Missile Crisis. The United States discovered that the Soviet Union was building nuclear missile sites in Cuba, just 90 miles from the U.S. mainland. President John F. Kennedy and his advisors were faced with the decision of how to respond.

The situation was incredibly tense, and there was no clear answer. Kennedy had to rely on his intuition, as well as the advice of his advisors, to navigate the crisis. He ultimately chose a naval blockade of Cuba, a decision that allowed for negotiations and eventually led to the de-escalation of the crisis.

The Cuban Missile Crisis is a prime example of the role of intuition in crisis decision-making. Kennedy's ability to trust his instincts, while also considering the input of his advisors, was crucial in avoiding a catastrophic outcome.

The Long-Term Impact of Crisis Leadership

The way a leader handles a crisis can have a lasting impact on both the team and the organization. Effective crisis leadership can strengthen bonds, build trust, and set a precedent for how future challenges are to be approached. Conversely, poor leadership during a crisis can lead to long-term damage, both to relationships and to the organization's reputation.

4.6.1 Building Trust and Loyalty

One of the most significant long-term impacts of effective crisis leadership is the trust and loyalty it can engender. When leaders guide their teams through a crisis with integrity, transparency, and empathy, they build a foundation of trust that can last well beyond the crisis itself.

Story: Rudy Giuliani and 9/11

When the terrorist attacks of September 11, 2001, struck New York City, Mayor Rudy Giuliani became the face of the city's response. His leadership during the crisis earned him widespread praise and significantly boosted his popularity.

Giuliani's handling of the crisis was marked by clear communication, visibility, and empathy. He was on the ground with first responders, comforting victims, and providing regular updates to the public. His leadership helped to reassure and unite the city during one of its darkest times.

The long-term impact of Giuliani's leadership during 9/11 was significant. He became known as "America's Mayor," and the trust and loyalty he built during the crisis continued to benefit him in his subsequent political career. However, it's worth noting that his reputation has since been affected by later actions, demonstrating that trust built during a crisis must be maintained through consistent leadership.

4.6.2 Setting a Precedent for Future Challenges

How a leader handles a crisis can set a precedent for how future challenges are approached. Leaders who demonstrate calm, effective crisis management can establish a culture of resilience and preparedness within their organization.

Story: The Johnson & Johnson Credo

The Tylenol crisis, mentioned earlier, not only salvaged the Tylenol brand but also reinforced Johnson & Johnson's corporate culture. The company's leadership, guided by the Johnson & Johnson Credo—a statement of the company's values—focused on the well-being of customers and acted quickly to address the crisis.

The way Johnson & Johnson handled the Tylenol crisis set a precedent for how the company would handle future challenges. The company's commitment to its Credo and its proactive approach to crisis management have become a model for other organizations.

The long-term impact of Johnson & Johnson's leadership during the Tylenol crisis is a powerful example of how effective crisis management can establish a lasting legacy of trust, integrity, and resilience.

Conclusion: The Role of Leadership in Shaping the Future

Leadership during a crisis is not just about navigating the immediate challenges—it's about shaping the future. The decisions made, the actions taken, and the example set during a crisis can have far-reaching implications for the team, the organization, and even society as a whole.

As we've seen throughout this chapter, effective leadership during a crisis requires a combination of courage, decisiveness, empathy, communication, and intuition. It's about finding the balance between making tough decisions and supporting your team, between acting quickly and considering the long-term impact.

Leaders who can navigate crises with these qualities not only help their teams survive the immediate challenges but also build a foundation for future success. They create a legacy of resilience, trust, and integrity that can guide their teams through whatever challenges may come next.

As we move forward in this book, we will continue to explore the strategies and principles that can help you become an effective crisis leader. By mastering the art of crisis leadership, you will be better equipped to guide your team through any storm and emerge stronger on the other side.

CHAPTER FIVE

The Power of Shared Goals

The success of any team or organization often hinges on its ability to rally around a set of shared goals. When individuals within a team align their efforts toward a common purpose, the collective energy becomes a powerful force, driving the group toward its objectives. This chapter delves into the concept of shared goals, exploring how they shape team dynamics, enhance collaboration, and contribute to long-term success. Through real-world examples, historical lessons, and practical strategies, we will see how shared goals can transform ordinary teams into extraordinary ones.

Understanding Shared Goals

Shared goals are the cornerstone of any successful team. These are objectives that every team member is committed to achieving. Unlike individual goals, which can vary widely and sometimes conflict, shared goals create a unified direction. When a team has a clear, collective aim, it fosters a sense of belonging and responsibility among its members.

5.1.1 The Nature of Shared Goals

Shared goals are more than just a list of targets. They embody the collective ambition of a team and reflect the values, mission, and vision of the organization. These goals are agreed upon by all team members, ensuring that everyone is on the same page. They are often broad, long-term objectives that require the collaboration of multiple people or departments.

For example, in a software development team, a shared goal might be to deliver a product by a specific deadline, with a particular set of features. Everyone in the team, from the developers to the testers to the product managers, is working toward that same outcome.

5.1.2 The Psychological Impact of Shared Goals

Shared goals have a profound psychological impact on team members. When people work toward a common goal, they feel a greater sense of purpose and motivation. This sense of purpose can enhance job satisfaction and lead to higher levels of engagement. Furthermore, when team members see their efforts contributing to a larger objective, they are more likely to experience a sense of accomplishment and pride in their work.

Story: The Apollo 11 Mission

One of the most compelling examples of the power of shared goals is the Apollo 11 mission. In 1961, President John F. Kennedy set a national goal of landing a man on the

Moon and returning him safely to Earth before the end of the decade. This goal was not just a technical challenge but a monumental collective ambition that required the efforts of thousands of individuals across multiple disciplines.

NASA's engineers, scientists, and astronauts were united by this shared goal. Despite numerous challenges, including technical failures and political pressures, the team's commitment to their common purpose never wavered. On July 20, 1969, Neil Armstrong became the first human to set foot on the Moon, a moment that marked the successful realization of a goal shared by an entire nation.

The Apollo 11 mission illustrates how a clear and compelling shared goal can galvanize a team, pushing them to overcome obstacles and achieve the seemingly impossible.

How Shared Goals Shape Team Dynamics

Shared goals are a critical factor in shaping team dynamics. They influence how team members interact, make decisions, and resolve conflicts. When a team is united by a common goal, it fosters collaboration, trust, and mutual support. Shared goals also help to clarify roles and responsibilities, ensuring that everyone knows what they need to do to contribute to the team's success.

5.2.1 Enhancing Collaboration

One of the most significant benefits of shared goals is that they enhance collaboration. When everyone is working towards the same objective, there is a natural tendency to support each other. Team members are more likely to share information, offer assistance, and collaborate on problem-solving.

Story: The Manhattan Project

During World War II, the United States embarked on the Manhattan Project, a secret research and development project aimed at creating the first nuclear weapons. The project brought together some of the greatest scientific minds of the time, including physicists like Robert Oppenheimer and Enrico Fermi.

The shared goal of developing a nuclear bomb before Nazi Germany created a unique environment of intense collaboration. Despite the secrecy and the enormous pressure, scientists from various disciplines worked together, sharing knowledge and overcoming technical challenges. The successful development of the atomic bomb, though controversial, demonstrated the immense power of collaboration driven by a shared goal.

The Manhattan Project underscores how a well-defined, urgent shared goal can unite individuals with diverse expertise, leading to groundbreaking achievements.

5.2.2 Building Trust and Accountability

Shared goals also play a crucial role in building trust and accountability within a team. When everyone is working toward the same objective, trust naturally develops as team members rely on each other to fulfill their responsibilities. This trust is further reinforced by a sense of accountability—each member knows that their contribution is vital to the team's success.

Example: Toyota's Production System

Toyota's production system, often referred to as "lean manufacturing," is another example of how shared goals can build trust and accountability within a team. The company's emphasis on continuous improvement (kaizen) and the elimination of waste is a shared goal across all levels of the organization.

Workers on the factory floor are empowered to stop the production line if they identify a problem, a practice known as "andon." This level of trust and accountability is possible because everyone shares the goal of producing the highest quality vehicles with the least waste. The shared commitment to this goal has made Toyota one of the most efficient and respected car manufacturers in the world.

Toyota's production system illustrates how shared goals can create a culture of trust and accountability, leading to consistent high performance.

The Role of Leadership in Establishing Shared Goals

Leadership plays a crucial role in establishing and reinforcing shared goals. It is the responsibility of leaders to articulate these goals clearly, align them with the organization's mission and vision, and ensure that all team members understand and commit to them. Effective leaders also inspire their teams to pursue these goals with passion and dedication.

5.3.1 Communicating the Vision

One of the most important tasks of a leader is to communicate the vision behind the shared goals. This involves explaining not only what the goals are but why they matter. When team members understand the significance of their work and how it contributes to the larger mission, they are more likely to be motivated and engaged.

Story: Martin Luther King Jr. and the Civil Rights Movement

Martin Luther King Jr. is an iconic example of a leader who effectively communicated a vision that galvanized a movement. His dream of a racially integrated society, where individuals would be judged by the content of their character rather than the color of their skin, became a shared goal for millions of Americans.

King's ability to articulate this vision in a way that resonated with people from all walks of life was a key factor in the success of the Civil Rights Movement. His speeches, particularly the famous "I Have a Dream" speech, inspired individuals to come together and work towards the shared goal of racial equality.

King's leadership demonstrates the power of a compelling vision in uniting people around shared goals, ultimately leading to profound social change.

5.3.2 Aligning Goals with Organizational Mission

Effective leaders also ensure that shared goals are aligned with the organization's mission and vision. When goals are connected to the broader purpose of the organization, they become more meaningful to team members. This alignment also helps to ensure that all efforts are directed towards achieving the long-term objectives of the organization.

Example: The Mission of SpaceX

SpaceX, the private aerospace company founded by Elon Musk, is driven by the mission of making space travel more affordable and ultimately enabling human life on Mars. This ambitious mission serves as the foundation for all the company's goals.

Every project at SpaceX, from developing reusable rockets to launching satellites, is aligned with the overarching goal of advancing space exploration and making human life multi-planetary. This alignment has not only motivated employees but has also attracted top talent from all around the world who share this vision.

SpaceX's success in revolutionizing space travel highlights the importance of aligning shared goals with a compelling organizational mission.

5.3.3 Inspiring Commitment

In addition to communicating the vision and aligning goals, leaders must also inspire commitment. This involves creating an environment where team members are passionate about their work and dedicated to achieving the shared goals. Leaders can inspire commitment by setting an example, recognizing and rewarding contributions, and fostering a culture of continuous improvement.

Story: Steve Jobs and Apple's Product Development

Steve Jobs, the co-founder of Apple, was known for his ability to inspire commitment among his team members. Jobs had a clear vision for Apple's products—he wanted them to be not only functional but also beautiful and user-friendly. This vision became a shared goal for everyone involved in product development.

Jobs' passion for excellence was contagious. He set high standards and pushed his team to innovate and achieve things that others thought were impossible. This relentless pursuit of perfection led to the creation of iconic products like the iPhone, iPad, and MacBook, which have had a profound impact on the technology industry.

Jobs' leadership at Apple demonstrates how inspiring commitment to shared goals can lead to groundbreaking achievements and lasting success.

The Impact of Shared Goals on Team Performance

Shared goals have a significant impact on team performance. When team members are united by common objectives, they are more likely to be focused, productive, and innovative. Shared goals also foster a sense of camaraderie and mutual support, which can lead to higher levels of job satisfaction and retention.

5.4.1 Improving Focus and Productivity

When a team has clear shared goals, it helps to focus their efforts and resources on what matters most. This focus can lead to increased productivity, as team members are less likely to be distracted by tasks that do not contribute to the shared objectives.

Example: Google's OKR System

Google is well-known for its use of the OKR (Objectives and Key Results) system, which is designed to set and track goals across the organization. The system encourages teams to establish ambitious objectives and identify measurable key results to achieve those objectives.

The shared goals set through the OKR system help to focus Google's teams on what is most important, ensuring that their efforts are aligned with the company's broader mission. This focus has contributed to Google's success as one of the most innovative and productive companies in the world.

Google's use of OKRs illustrates how shared goals can improve focus and productivity, leading to sustained success.

5.4.2 Fostering Innovation

Shared goals can also foster innovation by encouraging collaboration and creative problem-solving. When team members are working towards a common goal, they are more likely to share ideas, experiment with new approaches, and take calculated risks.

Story: The Development of Post-it Notes at 3M

The invention of Post-it Notes is a classic example of how shared goals can foster innovation. In the 1970s, 3M scientist Spencer Silver was trying to develop a strong adhesive, but instead created a weak one that could be easily removed. While this was initially seen as a failure, Silver shared his discovery with his colleague Art Fry, who was looking for a way to keep his bookmarks from falling out of his hymnal.

The shared goal of creating a useful product led to the development of Post-it Notes, which became one of 3M's most successful products. The collaborative effort between Silver and Fry, driven by the shared goal of solving a practical problem, demonstrates how innovation can emerge from unexpected places.

The story of Post-it Notes highlights how shared goals can lead to creative solutions and breakthrough innovations.

5.4.3 Enhancing Team Cohesion and Morale

Shared goals also enhance team cohesion and morale. When team members are working toward the same objectives, it creates a sense of unity and camaraderie. This shared purpose can lead to stronger relationships, increased trust, and a more positive work environment.

Example: The "Band of Brothers" in World War II

The "Band of Brothers" refers to the soldiers of Easy Company, 506th Parachute Infantry Regiment, 101st Airborne Division, who fought together during World War II. The shared goal of defeating the Axis powers and liberating Europe created a strong bond among these men, who came from diverse backgrounds.

Their shared experiences in combat, coupled with the collective goal of winning the war, forged deep and lasting friendships. The camaraderie and trust they developed were crucial to their success on the battlefield.

The story of the "Band of Brothers" illustrates how shared goals can enhance team cohesion and morale, leading to exceptional performance even in the most challenging circumstances.

Strategies for Creating and Maintaining Shared Goals

Establishing and maintaining shared goals is a dynamic process that requires careful planning, communication, and ongoing reinforcement. In this section, we will explore practical strategies for creating shared goals, keeping them aligned with the organization's mission, and ensuring that they remain relevant and motivating.

5.5.1 Involving the Team in Goal Setting

One of the most effective ways to create shared goals is to involve the team in the goal-setting process. When team members have a voice in defining the goals, they are more likely to feel a sense of ownership and commitment.

Example: Agile Methodologies

Agile methodologies, widely used in software development, emphasize the importance of involving the entire team in the planning process. In Agile, teams work together to define the goals for each sprint (a set period during which specific work must be completed). This collaborative approach ensures that everyone is aligned and invested in achieving the sprint's objectives.

The success of Agile methodologies in fostering collaboration and delivering high-quality software demonstrates the value of involving the team in goal setting.

5.5.2 Aligning Goals with Individual Strengths

To maximize the effectiveness of shared goals, it is important to align them with the individual strengths of team members. By assigning tasks and responsibilities that leverage each person's unique skills and expertise, leaders can ensure that the team is operating at its full potential.

Story: The Leadership of Mahatma Gandhi

Mahatma Gandhi's leadership during India's struggle for independence is an example of aligning goals with individual strengths. Gandhi understood that different people had different abilities and passions, so he encouraged them to contribute in ways that suited them best.

Some people were skilled in organizing non-violent protests, while others were effective in spreading the message of independence through writing, speeches, or community work. By aligning the shared goal of independence with individual strengths, Gandhi was able to build a diverse and effective movement that ultimately led to India's freedom.

Gandhi's leadership shows how aligning shared goals with individual strengths can lead to greater success and unity within a team.

5.5.3 Regularly Reviewing and Adjusting Goals

Shared goals should not be static; they need to be reviewed and adjusted regularly to ensure they remain relevant and aligned with the organization's evolving needs. This process of review and adjustment helps to keep the team focused and motivated.

Example: Amazon's Culture of Iteration

At Amazon, the concept of "working backwards" is central to the company's approach to goal setting. Teams start by envisioning the desired customer experience and then work backward to identify the steps needed to achieve that outcome. This process involves regular review and iteration of goals to ensure they remain aligned with customer needs and business objectives.

Amazon's culture of iteration and continuous improvement has been a key factor in its ability to innovate and maintain its position as a leader in the e-commerce industry.

The practice of regularly reviewing and adjusting goals helps to ensure that shared goals remain effective and aligned with the team's and organization's needs.

The Challenges of Maintaining Shared Goals

While shared goals are powerful tools for team success, maintaining them can be challenging. Teams may face obstacles such as conflicting priorities, changing circumstances, and communication breakdowns. In this section, we will explore some of these challenges and offer strategies for overcoming them.

5.6.1 Dealing with Conflicting Priorities

In any organization, there will be times when different teams or departments have conflicting priorities. These conflicts can undermine the effectiveness of shared goals if not addressed promptly and effectively.

Story: The Concorde Project

The development of the Concorde, the supersonic passenger jet, was a joint project between the British and French governments. While the shared goal was to create a groundbreaking aircraft, the project was plagued by conflicting priorities between the two countries, such as differing design preferences and budget constraints.

These conflicts led to delays, cost overruns, and ultimately limited the commercial success of the Concorde. The project highlights the importance of managing conflicting priorities when pursuing shared goals.

To overcome conflicting priorities, it is essential for leaders to facilitate open communication and negotiation, ensuring that all parties understand the importance of the shared goal and are willing to compromise when necessary.

5.6.2 Adapting to Changing Circumstances

In today's fast-paced business environment, circumstances can change rapidly, requiring teams to adapt their goals accordingly. Failure to adjust shared goals in response to new information or external factors can lead to misalignment and reduced effectiveness.

Example: Kodak's Decline

Kodak, once a dominant player in the photography industry, struggled to adapt to the digital revolution. The company's shared goals were initially focused on maintaining its leadership in film photography, but as the market shifted towards digital cameras, Kodak failed to adjust its goals on time.

This inability to adapt led to Kodak's decline and eventual bankruptcy. The company's experience serves as a cautionary tale about the importance of being flexible and responsive when circumstances change.

Leaders can help teams adapt to changing circumstances by encouraging a culture of agility and continuous learning, ensuring that shared goals remain relevant and achievable.

5.6.3 Overcoming Communication Barriers

Effective communication is essential for maintaining shared goals, but barriers such as geographical distance, cultural differences, and organizational silos can make it challenging. These barriers can lead to misunderstandings, misalignment, and decreased collaboration.

Story: The International Space Station (ISS)

The International Space Station (ISS) is a prime example of how communication barriers can be overcome to achieve a shared goal. The ISS is a collaborative project involving multiple countries, including the United States, Russia,

Japan, and several European nations.

Despite differences in language, culture and political interests, the teams involved in the ISS have successfully maintained open lines of communication, ensuring that everyone is aligned with the shared goal of advancing space research. The success of the ISS demonstrates that even the most complex communication barriers can be overcome with the right strategies and commitment.

Leaders can address communication barriers by promoting transparency, encouraging regular check-ins, and leveraging technology to facilitate collaboration across distances and cultures.

Conclusion: The Lasting Impact of Shared Goals

Shared goals are not just about achieving specific outcomes; they are about creating a sense of purpose, unity and resilience within a team. When team members are united by common objectives, they are more likely to support each other, innovate, and persevere in the face of challenges. The power of shared goals lies in their ability to transform a group of individuals into a cohesive, high-performing team that is capable of achieving great things.

As we have seen throughout this chapter, shared goals have played a pivotal role in some of history's most significant achievements, from the Apollo 11 mission to the Civil Rights Movement. These examples illustrate how shared goals can inspire collaboration, build trust and drive success, even in the most challenging circumstances.

In the next chapter, we will explore the importance of resilience in teams and how it can be cultivated through shared goals, strong leadership, and a supportive organizational culture. By understanding the role of resilience, leaders can better equip their teams to navigate the inevitable ups and downs of their journey toward shared success.

CHAPTER SIX

Lessons from Ancient Texts

In every culture, ancient texts carry profound wisdom that transcends time and geography. These texts often encapsulate the collective experience of civilizations, offering lessons that remain relevant even in contemporary times. In this chapter, we will explore how the teachings from Indian Epics like the Ramayana and Mahabharata, as well as from other ancient sources, provide insights into leadership, crisis management, and team dynamics.

We will also draw parallels between these ancient lessons and the leadership styles of some of the most prominent figures in modern history. By examining these connections, we can better understand how these timeless principles can be applied in today's corporate world to build resilient and cohesive teams.

The Ramayana: Leadership in the Face of Adversity

The Ramayana, one of India's most revered epics, is more than just a tale of gods, kings and battles. It is a profound exploration of duty, leadership and the moral dilemmas that leaders often face. Lord Rama, the protagonist, exemplifies the qualities of an ideal leader—integrity, compassion, and unwavering commitment to his responsibilities.

One of the most significant episodes in the Ramayana is the abduction of Sita, Lord Rama's wife, by the demon king Ravana. This event sets the stage for a crisis that tests Rama's leadership. Despite the personal pain and the overwhelming odds against him, Rama remains focused on his goal—to rescue Sita and restore dharma (righteousness). He builds alliances, leads a diverse group of followers, and strategically plans the assault on Lanka, Ravana's kingdom.

Real-Life Parallel: Rani Padmini's Valor

The story of Rani Padmini of Mewar mirrors the themes of duty and leadership under crisis depicted in the Ramayana. In the 13th century, Alauddin Khilji, the Sultan of Delhi, laid siege to the fortress of Chittorgarh, driven by his desire to capture the legendary beauty, Rani Padmini. Faced with an imminent threat, Rani Padmini and her followers displayed extraordinary courage and resolve. Rather than surrendering to Khilji, they chose to perform Jauhar (self-immolation) to protect their honor.

Rani Padmini's leadership in this dire situation is a powerful example of how leaders must sometimes make difficult, even tragic, decisions to uphold their values and protect their people. Her story, like that of Rama, underscores the importance of steadfastness, moral clarity, and the willingness to sacrifice for a greater cause.

Psychological Insight: Mental States in a Crisis

In both the Ramayana and the story of Rani Padmini, the leaders' mental states during the crisis are pivotal. According to crisis psychology, when faced with extreme stress, leaders often experience heightened alertness, focus, and a strong sense of purpose. This mental state, while challenging, can also lead to extraordinary acts of leadership. Both Rama and Rani Padmini demonstrate how maintaining composure and clarity of thought in a crisis can inspire and galvanize those they lead.

The Mahabharata: The Complexity of Leadership

The Mahabharata, another cornerstone of Indian literature, offers a more complex and nuanced view of leadership. The Epic is filled with characters who embody different aspects of leadership, from the righteous Yudhishthira to the ambitious Duryodhana and the enigmatic Krishna.

One of the central lessons of the Mahabharata is the concept of dharma—moral duty—which often conflicts with personal desires and practical considerations. The epic teaches that true leadership involves navigating these conflicts with wisdom and integrity.

Example: Arjuna and the Dilemma of Duty

Arjuna, one of the Pandava brothers, faces a profound crisis of conscience on the battlefield of Kurukshetra. As he stands ready to fight, he is overcome with doubt and despair at the thought of killing his own kin. It is in this moment of crisis that Krishna, his charioteer, delivers the

Bhagavad Gita, a discourse on duty, righteousness, and the nature of reality.

Krishna's counsel helps Arjuna overcome his paralysis and fulfill his duty as a warrior. This episode highlights the importance of moral clarity and the role of a leader in guiding others through ethical dilemmas.

Real-Life Parallel: Sardar Vallabhbhai Patel's Role in Uniting India

Sardar Vallabhbhai Patel, known as the "Iron Man of India," played a crucial role in the unification of India after independence. Faced with the enormous task of integrating more than 500 princely states into a single nation, Patel exhibited the same qualities of determination, pragmatism, and moral fortitude that Krishna espoused to Arjuna.

Patel's leadership was instrumental in persuading recalcitrant rulers to accede to India, often through tough negotiations and, when necessary, the use of force. His ability to navigate the complex political landscape of post-independence India, much like Krishna's guidance to Arjuna, ensured the stability and unity of the new nation.

Psychological Insight: Processing Information During a Crisis

In crises, leaders like Arjuna and Sardar Patel are required to process vast amounts of information quickly and make decisions under pressure. Cognitive psychologists suggest that during such times, the ability to filter relevant information, maintain focus, and avoid cognitive overload is crucial. Arjuna's moment of doubt and his subsequent clarity after Krishna's counsel illustrate how effective leadership involves not only decision-making but also managing one's mental state to remain effective.

The Bhagavad Gita: Ethical Leadership

The Bhagavad Gita, embedded within the Mahabharata, is one of the most important texts in Hindu philosophy. It addresses the moral and ethical challenges that leaders face and provides guidance on how to act with righteousness.

Example: The Concept of Nishkama Karma

One of the key teachings of the Gita is the concept of Nishkama Karma—performing one's duty without attachment to the results. Krishna advises Arjuna to act according to his dharma as a warrior, but without being attached to the outcomes of the battle. This principle is crucial for leaders who must often make decisions without being swayed by personal gain or fear of loss.

Real-Life Parallel: Dr. B.R. Ambedkar's Fight for Social Justice

Dr. B.R. Ambedkar, the chief architect of the Indian Constitution, exemplified the principle of Nishkama Karma in his lifelong struggle for the rights of the marginalized. Despite facing immense personal challenges and societal opposition, Ambedkar remained committed to his mission of social justice. His work in drafting a constitution that enshrined equality, freedom, and justice for all citizens, regardless of caste or creed, was driven by a sense of duty to the nation, rather than personal ambition.

Ambedkar's leadership, much like the teachings of the Gita, underscores the importance of ethical action and the pursuit of justice, regardless of the obstacles.

Psychological Insight: Behaviors in a Crisis

During crises, leaders often have to make decisions that may not yield immediate results, which can be psychologically taxing. The Gita's teachings on detachment from outcomes help leaders maintain their resolve and focus on their duties, even when the path ahead is fraught with uncertainty. This mindset can prevent burnout and ensure that leaders remain effective in the long run.

The Art of War: Strategic Leadership

Moving beyond Indian texts, The Art of War by Sun Tzu, an ancient Chinese military treatise, is another profound source of wisdom on leadership and strategy. Though it was written for the battlefield, its principles are applicable in all areas of leadership, especially in crisis situations.

Example: The Importance of Adaptability

One of Sun Tzu's key teachings is the importance of adaptability. He emphasizes that a leader must be flexible and responsive to changing circumstances, rather than rigidly adhering to a single plan.

Real-Life Parallel: Winston Churchill During World War II

Winston Churchill's leadership during World War II is a textbook example of adaptability in the face of crisis. When Britain stood alone against Nazi Germany, Churchill's ability to inspire resilience and adapt military strategies to the evolving situation was crucial to the Allied victory.

Churchill's leadership, characterized by his famous speeches and unyielding determination, mirrors Sun Tzu's advice on the importance of psychological warfare and maintaining the morale of one's own forces while destabilizing the enemy.

Psychological Insight: Negative Vicarious Rehearsal

Churchill's leadership also highlights the psychological concept of negative vicarious rehearsal—where individuals mentally simulate negative outcomes repeatedly, leading to increased anxiety and fear. Churchill was acutely aware of this phenomenon, both in himself and the British public, and used his speeches to counteract this by instilling a sense of hope and determination, which was critical in sustaining the nation's morale during the darkest days of the war.

Conclusion: Bridging Ancient Wisdom with Modern Leadership

The wisdom found in ancient texts like the Ramayana, Mahabharata, and The Art of War provides timeless guidance that transcends the eras they were written in. These stories are more than just historical or cultural relics—they are blueprints for leadership, offering insights into how to navigate crises, make ethical decisions, and lead with integrity.

The lessons from these texts remind us that true leadership is not merely about making strategic decisions; it is about embodying core values, guiding teams through moral complexities, and maintaining composure in the face of adversity. These principles have been exemplified by great leaders throughout history, such as Rani Padmini, Sardar Vallabhbhai Patel, Dr. B.R. Ambedkar, and Winston Churchill, who faced challenges that tested their resolve and defined their leadership.

In our contemporary world, where challenges are often unpredictable and complex, the teachings from these ancient texts remain profoundly relevant. By integrating these time-honored principles into modern leadership practices, we can cultivate resilience, ethical clarity, and the ability to inspire and unite our teams even in the most challenging circumstances.

CHAPTER SEVEN

Learning from Great Leaders

Great leaders are often forged in the crucible of crisis. Their actions, decisions, and strategies during times of uncertainty not only shape the outcomes of those crises but also leave an enduring legacy. In this chapter, we will explore the leadership lessons drawn from the lives of some of history's most influential figures, understanding how they navigated complex challenges and used crises as opportunities to build stronger, more cohesive teams.

This chapter will delve into the lives and leadership styles of figures like Jawaharlal Nehru, Dr. B.R. Ambedkar, Mahatma Gandhi, Nelson Mandela, Winston Churchill, and many more. By analyzing their approaches, we can extract practical lessons that are applicable to modern leadership, especially in the context of crisis management.

Jawaharlal Nehru: Visionary Leadership in the Face of Adversity

Jawaharlal Nehru, India's first Prime Minister, was a leader who faced immense challenges from the very beginning of his tenure. Post-independence India was a nation marked by partition, communal violence, and widespread poverty. Nehru's leadership was instrumental in steering the country through these turbulent times and laying the foundations for modern India.

Nehru's vision of a secular, socialist, and democratic India was not just a political stance; it was a blueprint for nation-building. His ability to maintain a clear and long-term vision amidst immediate crises was one of his greatest strengths. For instance, when India was partitioned in 1947, Nehru had to manage not only the division of the country but also the massive displacement and violence that followed. His response was not just to address the immediate humanitarian crisis but to also focus on long-term solutions, such as establishing institutions of higher learning like the Indian Institutes of Technology (IITs) and Indian Institutes of Management (IIMs) to foster scientific and managerial talent in the country.

Example: The Kashmir Crisis

One of the most significant crises Nehru faced was the Kashmir conflict. Shortly after independence, the princely state of Jammu and Kashmir became a flashpoint between India and Pakistan. Nehru's leadership during this period was marked by a careful balancing act. He had to navigate international diplomacy, military strategy, and the aspirations of the Kashmiri people. His decision to take the matter to the United Nations, though controversial, was guided by his commitment to resolving the issue through peaceful means, a principle that he held dear throughout his life.

Lesson:

Nehru's leadership teaches us the importance of having a clear vision and sticking to core values, even during crises. Leaders should be able to look beyond immediate challenges and make decisions that align with their long-term goals and principles. His ability to balance immediate needs with long-term vision is a crucial lesson for modern leaders.

Dr. B.R. Ambedkar: Leadership in the Struggle for Social Justice

Dr. B.R. Ambedkar, a key architect of the Indian Constitution, was a leader who turned personal adversity into a driving force for social change. Born into a Dalit family, Ambedkar faced systemic discrimination and exclusion throughout his life. However, instead of succumbing to these challenges, he used them as a catalyst to fight for the rights of the marginalized and oppressed.

Ambedkar's leadership during the drafting of the Indian Constitution is a prime example of his ability to lead through a crisis. The challenge of uniting a diverse and divided nation under a common legal framework was immense. Ambedkar's deep understanding of social issues, combined with his legal acumen, enabled him to draft a constitution that not only safeguarded individual rights but also laid the foundation for social justice.

Example: The Hindu Code Bill

One of Ambedkar's significant contributions was his advocacy for the Hindu Code Bill, which sought to reform

Hindu personal law to promote gender equality. The bill faced stiff opposition from orthodox sections of society, and Ambedkar had to navigate intense political and social pressure. Despite the bill not being passed in his time, his efforts paved the way for future reforms that significantly improved the status of women in India.

Lesson:

Ambedkar's leadership exemplifies the power of resilience and the importance of standing up for what is right, even in the face of overwhelming opposition. His life is a testament to the fact that crises can be opportunities to challenge the status quo and bring about meaningful change. Leaders must have the courage to confront difficult issues head-on and the perseverance to see their vision through to fruition.

Mahatma Gandhi: The Power of Non-Violent Resistance

Mahatma Gandhi's leadership during India's struggle for independence is perhaps one of the most studied and revered examples of leadership in the face of crisis. Gandhi's approach to leadership was rooted in the principles of non-violence (ahimsa) and truth (satya), which he used as powerful tools to mobilize millions of Indians against British colonial rule.

Gandhi's ability to galvanize a nation through peaceful means was not just a political strategy but a deeply moral stance. His leadership was tested during several crises, including the Non-Cooperation Movement, the Civil Disobedience Movement, and the Quit India Movement. In each instance, Gandhi's commitment to non-violence remained steadfast, even when faced with brutal repression from the British authorities.

Example: The Salt March

The Salt March of 1930 is one of the most iconic examples of Gandhi's leadership. The British government had imposed a tax on salt, a staple in every Indian household. Gandhi's decision to march 240 miles to the coastal village of Dandi to produce salt from seawater was a direct challenge to British authority. This act of civil disobedience sparked widespread protests across the country and highlighted the power of non-violent resistance.

Lesson:

Gandhi's leadership teaches us that moral conviction can be a powerful force for change. His ability to inspire collective action through non-violent means shows that leaders do not always need to rely on force or coercion to achieve their goals. Instead, they can draw on the power of principles and values to unite people and bring about transformative change.

Nelson Mandela: Forging Unity from Division

Nelson Mandela's leadership during South Africa's transition from apartheid to democracy is a profound example of leading through crisis. Mandela spent 27 years in prison for his fight against apartheid, and when he was finally released, he faced the monumental task of uniting a deeply divided nation.

Mandela's leadership was characterized by his emphasis on reconciliation rather than retribution. Despite the decades of oppression and violence that he and his people had endured, Mandela chose to focus on healing the nation rather than seeking revenge. His leadership during this critical period was instrumental in preventing South Africa from descending into civil war and instead transitioning into a peaceful democracy.

Example: The Truth and Reconciliation Commission

One of Mandela's most significant initiatives was the establishment of the Truth and Reconciliation Commission (TRC). The TRC was tasked with investigating human rights abuses that occurred during the apartheid era. Rather than seeking to punish the perpetrators, the commission focused on uncovering the truth and promoting forgiveness and reconciliation. Mandela's support for the TRC was a clear indication of his belief in the power of forgiveness as a means of healing a nation.

Lesson:

Mandela's leadership underscores the importance of forgiveness and reconciliation in the aftermath of a crisis. His ability to look beyond personal grievances and focus on the greater good of the nation is a critical lesson for leaders today. In times of crisis, leaders must be willing to put aside personal or partisan interests to promote unity and start healing within their teams and communities.

Winston Churchill: Leadership in Times of War

Winston Churchill, the British Prime Minister during World War II, is often cited as one of the greatest wartime leaders of the 20th century. Churchill's leadership during the darkest days of the war, particularly during the Battle of Britain, was marked by his unyielding determination and his ability to inspire a nation under siege.

Churchill's speeches and public addresses played a crucial role in bolstering the morale of the British people during the war. His famous speeches, such as "We shall fight on the beaches" and "Their finest hour," are remembered for their defiance and their ability to rally the nation behind the war effort. Churchill's leadership during this period was not just about military strategy; it was about giving hope to a nation facing existential threats.

Example: The Dunkirk Evacuation

One of Churchill's most challenging moments as a leader was the evacuation of British and Allied troops from Dunkirk in 1940. With the German army advancing, the situation seemed dire. However, Churchill's leadership was instrumental in organizing the evacuation, which saved over 300,000 soldiers. His decision to frame the evacuation as a "miracle of deliverance" rather than a defeat helped to maintain public morale and solidify his reputation as a steadfast leader.

Lesson:

Churchill's leadership teaches us the importance of resilience and the power of communication during crises. His ability to inspire confidence and maintain public morale, even in the face of overwhelming odds, is a crucial lesson for modern leaders. In times of crisis, leaders must be able to communicate effectively, instilling hope and confidence in their teams.

Rani Padmini: The Courage of Leadership in Crisis

Rani Padmini, the legendary queen of Mewar, is remembered for her unwavering courage and leadership during one of the most challenging crises in Indian history. When Alauddin Khilji, the Sultan of Delhi, laid siege to the fortress of Chittorgarh, Rani Padmini was faced with an impossible situation. Khilji was determined to capture her, driven by both political ambition and personal obsession.

Rather than surrendering or allowing herself to be captured, Rani Padmini made the ultimate sacrifice. She chose to lead the women of Chittorgarh in performing Jauhar, an ancient Rajput tradition of self-immolation, to protect their honor from the invaders. This act of mass self-sacrifice is seen as a symbol of Rajput pride and resistance against tyranny.

Lesson:

While Rani Padmini's story is rooted in a different cultural and historical context, her leadership during this crisis highlights the importance of courage and the willingness to make difficult decisions for the greater good. Modern leaders can learn from her example the value of protecting the integrity and dignity of their teams, even in the face of overwhelming adversity.

Sardar Vallabhbhai Patel: The Iron Man of India

Sardar Vallabhbhai Patel, known as the Iron Man of India, played a pivotal role in uniting the newly independent country. After India gained independence in 1947, it was a fragmented nation with over 500 princely states, each with its own rulers and agendas. Patel's leadership was crucial in integrating these states into the Indian Union, a task that required both diplomacy and, at times, the use of force.

Example: The Integration of Hyderabad

One of the most challenging situations Patel faced was the integration of the princely state of Hyderabad. The Nizam of Hyderabad, one of the richest rulers in the world at the time, was reluctant to join the Indian Union and sought to remain independent. Patel's leadership during this crisis was marked by his firm resolve and strategic acumen. When negotiations failed, Patel authorized a military operation, codenamed Operation Polo, to annex Hyderabad into India. The operation was swift and effective, and Hyderabad became a part of the Indian Union without significant bloodshed.

Lesson:

Patel's leadership exemplifies the importance of firmness and strategic thinking in crisis situations. His ability to balance diplomacy with decisive action is a valuable lesson for leaders who must navigate complex challenges while maintaining the unity and stability of their teams or organizations.

Franklin D. Roosevelt: Leading Through Economic Crisis

Franklin D. Roosevelt (FDR), the 32nd President of the United States, is best known for his leadership during two of the most significant crises of the 20th century: the Great Depression and World War II. When FDR took office in 1933, the United States was in the depths of the Great Depression, with unemployment rates soaring and the economy in shambles. Roosevelt's leadership during this period was characterized by his bold and innovative approach to crisis management.

Example: The New Deal

FDR's New Deal was a series of programs and policies designed to provide relief, recovery, and reform during the Great Depression. These initiatives included the creation of social security, unemployment insurance, and various public works programs that provided jobs and stimulated economic growth. FDR's leadership during this period was marked by his willingness to experiment with different solutions and his ability to communicate his vision to the American people, restoring their confidence in the government and the economy.

Lesson:

Roosevelt's leadership teaches us the importance of adaptability and innovation in the face of crisis. His willingness to try new approaches and his ability to communicate effectively with the public were key to his success in leading the nation out of the Great Depression. Modern leaders can learn from FDR's example the value of being open to new ideas and maintaining clear and transparent communication with their teams during times of uncertainty.

Margaret Thatcher: The Power of Resolve in Leadership

Margaret Thatcher, the first female Prime Minister of the United Kingdom, is often referred to as the "Iron Lady" for her strong-willed leadership. Thatcher's time in office was marked by significant challenges, including economic recession, widespread industrial unrest, and the Falklands War. Her leadership during these crises was characterized by her unwavering resolve and her commitment to her principles.

Example: The Falklands War

In 1982, Argentina invaded the Falkland Islands, a British territory in the South Atlantic. Thatcher's decision to send a naval task force to retake the islands was a bold and risky move, but it demonstrated her determination to defend British sovereignty. The successful recapture of the Falklands not only bolstered Thatcher's leadership but also restored national pride in the United Kingdom.

Lesson:

Thatcher's leadership during the Falklands War highlights the importance of resolve and decisiveness in leadership. Her ability to stand firm in the face of adversity and take bold action when necessary is a crucial lesson for leaders who must navigate complex and high-stakes situations.

Abraham Lincoln: Leadership in the Midst of Civil War

Abraham Lincoln, the 16th President of the United States, is often celebrated for his leadership during one of the most challenging periods in American history—the Civil War. Lincoln's leadership was marked by his deep commitment to preserving the Union and his moral conviction to end slavery.

Example: The Emancipation Proclamation

One of Lincoln's most significant actions as a leader was the issuance of the Emancipation Proclamation in 1863. This executive order declared the freedom of all slaves in Confederate-held territory. While it did not immediately free all slaves, it was a crucial step towards the abolition of slavery and shifted the focus of the war to a moral cause. Lincoln's leadership during the Civil War was characterized by his ability to balance pragmatism with moral conviction, leading the nation through its darkest hour and ultimately preserving the Union.

Lesson:

Lincoln's leadership teaches us the importance of moral clarity and the ability to navigate complex and divided situations with both compassion and firmness. His example is a reminder that leaders must sometimes make difficult decisions that may not be immediately popular but are necessary for the greater good.

Conclusion

The stories of these great leaders illustrate that leadership in crisis is not about having all the answers but about navigating uncertainty with a clear vision, strong values, and the ability to inspire and unite others. Each of these leaders faced immense challenges, yet their responses to these crises not only defined their legacies but also left an indelible mark on history.

From Nehru's visionary leadership in post-independence India to Mandela's emphasis on reconciliation, from Gandhi's non-violent resistance to Churchill's defiance during war, these leaders offer timeless lessons for anyone who aspires to lead in times of crisis. By studying their lives and actions, we can gain valuable insights into the qualities and strategies that make for effective leadership, even in the most challenging circumstances.

As we face the inevitable crises that come our way, whether in our personal lives, our organizations, or our communities, we can draw strength and inspiration from these great leaders. Their examples remind us that crises, while challenging, also present opportunities for growth, transformation, and the creation of a legacy that endures long after the crisis has passed.

CHAPTER EIGHT

Implementing a Crisis-Driven Team Building Strategy

In this chapter, we delve into the practical steps of implementing a crisis-driven team-building strategy. This approach is not just about reacting to crises but about proactively creating an environment where challenges are used as opportunities to strengthen team cohesion, align with the company's vision, and drive success. We will explore real-life examples from various industries and leaders who have successfully utilized crises to build resilient and high-performing teams.

Understanding the Nature of Crises

Crises come in many forms—financial downturns, unexpected market shifts, technological disruptions, and even internal conflicts. Each crisis brings unique challenges, but they all share a common feature: they disrupt the status quo. This disruption creates a window of opportunity where team dynamics can be reshaped, and stronger bonds can be forged.

For example, in the early 2000s, IBM faced a significant crisis as it struggled to transition from a hardware-focused company to a services-oriented one. Under the leadership of CEO Lou Gerstner, the company embraced this challenge. Gerstner encouraged open communication, transparency, and a shared sense of purpose among employees. The crisis became a catalyst for change, uniting the team around a common goal of transforming IBM into a leading services company. This shift not only saved the company but also set it on a path to sustained success.

Step 1: Cultivate a Crisis-Ready Mindset

The first step in implementing a crisis-driven team-building strategy is to cultivate a mindset that views crises as opportunities rather than threats. This requires a shift in perspective at all levels of the organization. Leaders must communicate the potential benefits of crises and encourage their teams to embrace challenges with resilience and creativity.

Example: NASA's Apollo 13 Mission

One of the most famous examples of a crisis-driven mindset is NASA's handling of the Apollo 13 mission. When an oxygen tank exploded two days into the mission, it seemed impossible that the crew would return safely to Earth. However, NASA's team, led by Flight Director Gene Kranz, refused to see the situation as a failure. Instead, they focused on finding solutions. The crisis united the team, leading to innovative problem-solving under immense pressure. The successful return of the astronauts became a testament to the power of a crisis-driven mindset.

Step 2: Foster Open Communication

During a crisis, clear and open communication is crucial. Team members need to be informed about the situation, the challenges ahead, and the roles they are expected to play. Leaders must encourage transparency and create a safe space for team members to express concerns, share ideas, and collaborate on solutions.

Example: Johnson & Johnson's Tylenol Crisis

In 1982, Johnson & Johnson faced a severe crisis when several people died after taking Tylenol capsules laced with cyanide. The company's response, led by then-CEO James Burke, is still studied as a model of effective crisis management. Burke immediately prioritized open communication, both internally and externally. He kept employees informed, involved them in decision-making, and maintained transparency with the public. This approach not only resolved the crisis but also reinforced trust in the company and strengthened the team's commitment to its values.

Step 3: Align with a Shared Vision

Crises provide an opportunity to realign teams with the organization's mission and vision. Leaders should use the crisis as a moment to reiterate the company's goals and how overcoming the current challenge will contribute to long-term success. This alignment helps teams stay focused and motivated, even in the face of adversity.

Example: Apple's Near Bankruptcy in the 1990s

In the late 1990s, Apple was on the brink of bankruptcy. When Steve Jobs returned to the company, he used the crisis as an opportunity to refocus the team on innovation and simplicity. Jobs communicated a clear vision: to make great products that people love. This shared goal rallied the team, leading to the development of iconic products like the iMac, iPod, and iPhone. The crisis not only saved Apple but also transformed it into one of the most successful companies in the world.

Step 4: Empower Teams to Innovate

Crises often require quick thinking and innovative solutions. Leaders should empower their teams to take initiative, experiment with new ideas, and develop creative solutions. This not only helps resolve the immediate crisis but also fosters a culture of innovation that can benefit the organization in the long term.

Example: The Creation of Slack

Slack, now a leading communication platform, was born out of a crisis. Stewart Butterfield and his team were working on a game called Glitch, which ultimately failed to gain traction. Faced with the failure of their primary project, the team pivoted to develop an internal communication tool they had created to collaborate on Glitch. This tool became Slack. The crisis forced the team to innovate, leading to the creation of a product that transformed workplace communication globally.

Step 5: Build Trust Through Shared Experiences

One of the most powerful outcomes of navigating a crisis together is the deepening of trust among team members. When people work together to overcome significant challenges, they build bonds that can withstand future pressures. Leaders should recognize and celebrate these shared experiences as milestones in the team's journey.

Example: The Chilean Mining Rescue

In 2010, 33 Chilean miners were trapped underground for 69 days after a cave-in. The rescue operation involved collaboration between the miners, their families, the Chilean government, and international experts. The shared experience of overcoming this life-and-death crisis forged strong bonds among all involved. The miners' teamwork and resilience were critical to their survival, and the trust built during this ordeal has been highlighted in numerous studies as an example of crisis-driven team building.

Step 6: Reinforce Lessons Learned

After a crisis, it's important to take time to reflect on the experience and reinforce the lessons learned. Leaders should conduct debriefings with their teams, discussing what worked, what didn't, and how similar situations can be handled in the future. This reflection solidifies the team's growth and prepares them for future challenges.

Example: Toyota's Response to the 2011 Earthquake and Tsunami

The 2011 earthquake and tsunami in Japan severely disrupted Toyota's supply chain. The crisis forced the company to rethink its operations, leading to the development of more resilient systems. After the crisis, Toyota conducted thorough reviews to understand the lessons learned. These debriefings not only improved the company's crisis response but also strengthened the team's ability to collaborate and innovate under pressure.

Step 7: Institutionalize Crisis-Driven Practices

Finally, organizations should institutionalize the practices that helped them navigate the crisis successfully. This means embedding crisis-driven team building into the company's culture, processes, and leadership development programs. By doing so, organizations ensure that they are always prepared to turn challenges into opportunities.

Example: The U.S. Military's After-Action Reviews (AARs)

The U.S. military has institutionalized the practice of After-Action Reviews (AARs) to learn from every mission, whether successful or not. These reviews involve a candid discussion of what happened, why it happened, and how it can be improved. The AAR process has been adopted by many organizations as a way to institutionalize learning from crises and reinforce a culture of continuous improvement and resilience.

Real-Life Case Study: Netflix's Reinvention

Netflix provides a powerful example of a company that has institutionalized crisis-driven practices. In the early 2000s, Netflix faced a significant crisis when its DVD rental business began to decline due to the rise of online streaming. Instead of viewing this as a threat, CEO Reed Hastings saw it as an opportunity to transform the company. Netflix pivoted to become a streaming service, and later, a content creator. This strategic shift was not without challenges, but the company's willingness to embrace crisis-driven innovation allowed it to thrive in a rapidly changing industry. Netflix's success today can be attributed to its ability to institutionalize a culture of agility, innovation, and resilience.

Conclusion: Embracing the Crisis-Driven Approach

Implementing a crisis-driven team-building strategy is not about waiting for a disaster to strike. It's about fostering a culture where challenges are seen as opportunities for growth, where teams are empowered to innovate, and where shared experiences build trust and resilience. By following the steps outlined in this chapter, leaders can create an environment where crises become catalysts for building stronger, more cohesive, and more successful teams.

As we've seen from the real-life examples and stories shared in this chapter, the crisis-driven approach is a powerful tool for transforming teams and organizations.

It requires a shift in mindset, a commitment to open communication, and a focus on shared goals. But the rewards—stronger teams, greater innovation, and long-term success—are well worth the effort.

By embracing this approach, leaders can not only navigate crises more effectively but also build teams that are more aligned, resilient, and capable of achieving extraordinary results.

Measuring Success

Success is a word that often evokes different images and expectations in people's minds. For some, success might be financial gain, for others, it could be a personal sense of accomplishment. When it comes to team building, especially through the lens of crisis-driven strategies, measuring success becomes both a quantitative and qualitative endeavor. In this chapter, we explore how to measure success after implementing crisis-driven team-building strategies, focusing on both the tangible and intangible outcomes. We'll delve into real-world examples, with a special emphasis on Indian stories, to provide a comprehensive guide on assessing the effectiveness of these strategies.

The Need for Clear Metrics

Before diving into specific examples, it's crucial to establish the importance of clear metrics when measuring success. Without defined criteria, success becomes an abstract concept, subject to interpretation and often leading to inconsistent outcomes. Metrics provide a concrete way to evaluate the impact of crisis-driven strategies on team cohesion, productivity, and overall organizational health.

Example: The Green Revolution in India

One of the most significant examples of using clear metrics to measure success can be drawn from India's Green Revolution in the 1960s and 1970s. Faced with a potential food crisis due to population growth and stagnating agricultural production, the Indian government, led by Prime Minister Lal Bahadur Shastri and later Indira Gandhi, implemented a series of agricultural reforms. The success of these reforms was measured through clear metrics—crop yields, food production levels, and reduction in food imports.

The Green Revolution was a success not just because of the increase in crop yields but because these metrics allowed the government to monitor progress, make adjustments, and ultimately transform India from a food-deficient country to a food-surplus one. This example illustrates the power of clear metrics in assessing the success of a crisis-driven strategy.

Quantitative Measures of Success

Quantitative measures are essential for providing concrete evidence of success. These include metrics such as productivity levels, financial performance, employee retention rates, and customer satisfaction scores. These metrics can be tracked over time to determine the impact of crisis-driven team-building strategies.

Example: Tata Group's Response to the 2008 Global Financial Crisis

During the 2008 global financial crisis, many companies faced severe financial strain. The Tata Group, one of India's largest conglomerates, was no exception. However, under the leadership of Ratan Tata, the company implemented several crisis-driven strategies to maintain stability and growth. One of the key metrics used to measure success was the company's financial performance, particularly its ability to sustain profitability during a period of global economic downturn.

By focusing on cost management, restructuring operations, and investing in core businesses, Tata Group was able to not only survive the crisis but also emerge stronger. The company's financial metrics—such as revenue growth, profit margins, and return on investment—provided clear evidence of the success of its crisis-driven strategies.

Qualitative Measures of Success

While quantitative metrics are essential, they often don't capture the full picture. Qualitative measures, such as employee morale, team cohesion, and leadership effectiveness, are equally important in assessing the success of crisis-driven strategies. These measures provide insights into the intangible aspects of success that are critical for long-term organizational health.

Example: Infosys and the Leadership Crisis of 2017

In 2017, Infosys, one of India's leading IT services companies, faced a leadership crisis when CEO Vishal Sikka resigned amid tensions with the company's founders and board. This crisis had the potential to destabilize the company, but under the interim leadership of U.B. Pravin Rao and later Salil Parekh, Infosys managed to navigate the situation effectively.

The success of their approach wasn't just measured in financial terms but also in qualitative aspects such as employee morale and leadership trust. The company conducted internal surveys to assess employee sentiment, held town hall meetings to address concerns, and focused on rebuilding trust within the organization. The qualitative feedback from these efforts indicated a significant improvement in team cohesion and morale, which were crucial in stabilizing the company during a turbulent period.

Balancing Short-Term and Long-Term Success

One of the challenges in measuring success is balancing short-term gains with long-term sustainability. Crisis-driven strategies often yield immediate results, but it's important to ensure that these strategies also contribute to long-term success. This requires a dual focus on immediate metrics and forward-looking indicators.

Example: The Success of ISRO's Mars Orbiter Mission (Mangalyaan)

India's Mars Orbiter Mission, also known as Mangalyaan, is a prime example of balancing short-term and long-term success. Launched in 2013 by the Indian Space Research Organisation (ISRO), Mangalyaan was India's first interplanetary mission and was successfully inserted into Mars' orbit in 2014. The mission was accomplished on a shoestring budget, making it a significant short-term success.

However, ISRO didn't just measure success by the mission's immediate achievements. They also looked at long-term indicators such as the mission's contribution to scientific research, the development of new technologies, and the enhancement of India's reputation in the global space community. By balancing these short-term and long-term measures, ISRO was able to not only achieve immediate success but also lay the groundwork for future missions and advancements in space technology.

Learning from Failures

An often overlooked but critical aspect of measuring success is learning from failures. Not all crisis-driven strategies will succeed, and it's important to analyze and understand the reasons behind failures. This learning process is essential for refining strategies and ensuring future success.

Example: Kingfisher Airlines' Downfall

Kingfisher Airlines, once one of India's most prominent airlines, provides a stark example of the importance of learning from failures. The airline, owned by Vijay Mallya, expanded rapidly in the mid-2000s, but by 2012, it was grounded due to financial difficulties, poor management decisions, and an inability to manage crisis effectively.

While the airline's downfall was a failure, it offers valuable lessons in crisis management and the importance of sustainable growth. The lack of clear metrics to monitor financial health, coupled with a failure to adapt to changing market conditions, led to the airline's collapse. This example underscores the importance of learning from failures and using those lessons to build more robust strategies in the future.

The Role of Continuous Feedback and Improvement

Measuring success is not a one-time activity but an ongoing process. Continuous feedback and improvement are essential for ensuring that crisis-driven strategies remain effective over time. This involves regularly reviewing metrics, soliciting feedback from team members, and making necessary adjustments to strategies.

Example: Flipkart's Evolution in the E-Commerce Market

Flipkart, one of India's leading e-commerce platforms, has continuously evolved its strategies to stay competitive in a rapidly changing market. Founded in 2007 by Sachin and Binny Bansal, Flipkart faced numerous challenges, including competition from global giants like Amazon.

One of the key factors behind Flipkart's success has been its commitment to continuous feedback and improvement. The company regularly reviews its performance metrics, customer feedback, and market trends to refine its strategies. This approach allowed Flipkart to navigate crises such as intense competition, regulatory challenges, and market fluctuations while maintaining its position as a market leader. The company's ability to adapt and improve continuously is a testament to the effectiveness of this approach.

Using Success Stories to Reinforce Team Morale

Success stories play a crucial role in reinforcing team morale and sustaining momentum. Celebrating successes, whether big or small, helps to build a positive organizational culture and encourages teams to continue striving for excellence.

Example: The Success of TCS's Digital Transformation Initiatives

Tata Consultancy Services (TCS), one of India's largest IT services companies, successfully undertook a digital transformation journey in the early 2010s. Faced with the challenge of adapting to a rapidly changing technology landscape, TCS implemented several initiatives to upskill its workforce, innovate in service delivery, and expand its digital offerings.

The success of these initiatives was celebrated across the organization, with leaders sharing stories of teams that had achieved remarkable results. These success stories were not only recognized internally but also shared with clients and stakeholders, reinforcing TCS's reputation as a leader in digital transformation. This approach helped boost employee morale and motivated teams to continue pushing the boundaries of innovation.

Building a Culture of Accountability

Accountability is a key component of measuring success. Teams and leaders must be held accountable for the outcomes of their crisis-driven strategies. This accountability ensures that everyone is committed to the success of the initiative and is willing to take ownership of both successes and failures.

Example: The Accountability Framework in the Indian Railways

The Indian Railways, one of the largest railway networks in the world, has implemented several initiatives to improve safety, efficiency, and customer service. One of the critical aspects of these initiatives has been the establishment of a robust accountability framework.

For example, after a series of accidents in the early 2010s, the Indian Railways introduced measures to improve safety, including regular audits, enhanced training for staff, and stricter enforcement of safety protocols. Accountability was a central theme, with clear metrics for safety performance and a commitment to holding responsible parties accountable for any lapses. This framework has contributed to significant improvements in safety and operational efficiency across the network.

The Importance of Stakeholder Alignment

Success is often measured not just by internal metrics but also by the satisfaction of external stakeholders, including customers, investors, and partners. Ensuring alignment with stakeholder expectations is crucial for long-term success.

Example: The Success of Amul's Cooperative Model

Amul, one of India's largest dairy cooperatives, is a prime example of stakeholder alignment. Founded in 1946, Amul operates on a cooperative model where farmers are the primary stakeholders. The success of Amul's crisis-driven strategies, such as the White Revolution, has been measured not just by the company's financial performance but also by the improved livelihoods of its farmer-members.

Amul's success is reflected in the satisfaction of its stakeholders—farmers receive fair prices for their milk, consumers get high-quality dairy products, and the cooperative continues to grow and expand. This alignment with stakeholder expectations has been key to Amul's sustained success over the decades.

Developing a Long-Term Vision for Success

Finally, measuring success requires a long-term vision. Crisis-driven strategies should not only address immediate challenges but also contribute to the organization's long-term goals. This requires a clear understanding of what success looks like in the future and how current strategies align with that vision.

Example: Mahindra Group's Vision 2025

The Mahindra Group, one of India's largest conglomerates, has a long-term vision known as Vision 2025. This vision focuses on becoming a globally admired brand, achieving leadership in key sectors, and driving positive change in the communities it serves. The success of Mahindra's crisis-driven strategies is measured not just by short-term financial performance but by progress towards this long-term vision.

For example, Mahindra's foray into electric vehicles (EVs) is part of its long-term vision for sustainable mobility. Despite challenges in the EV market, Mahindra has remained committed to its vision, measuring success through milestones such as product launches, market penetration, and contributions to environmental sustainability. This long-term perspective ensures that crisis-driven strategies are aligned with the company's overarching goals.

Conclusion: The Multifaceted Nature of Success

Measuring success in the context of crisis-driven team-building strategies is a multifaceted process. It involves a combination of quantitative and qualitative metrics, a balance between short-term and long-term goals, and a commitment to continuous improvement and accountability. By learning from both successes and failures, celebrating achievements, and aligning with stakeholder expectations, organizations can ensure that their crisis-driven strategies not only address immediate challenges but also contribute to sustained success.

As we have seen from the Indian examples and stories shared in this chapter, success is not a one-size-fits-all concept. It requires a nuanced approach that takes into account the unique context of each organization and the specific challenges it faces. By adopting a holistic approach to measuring success, leaders can build stronger, more resilient teams that are capable of navigating crises and achieving extraordinary results in the long term.

CHAPTER TEN

Moving Forward

As we reach the final chapter of this book, the concept of crisis-driven team building has been explored from various angles—starting from understanding the role of crises in team dynamics, drawing lessons from ancient texts, learning from great leaders, and implementing strategies that turn challenges into opportunities. Now, the question that remains is: How do we move forward? How do we sustain the momentum built during a crisis, and how do we continue to evolve as leaders and as teams?

Moving forward is about embedding the lessons learned during crises into the fabric of our organizations. It's about ensuring that the strategies and practices we've developed don't just fade away once the crisis is over but become a part of the organizational culture. This chapter will delve into how to achieve this, using real-world examples, with a special focus on Indian stories, to provide a comprehensive guide on sustaining and building upon the success achieved through crisis-driven team building.

Embedding Crisis Lessons into Organizational Culture

One of the most important steps in moving forward is to embed the lessons learned during crises into the organizational culture. This means making crisis-driven strategies a part of the everyday functioning of the organization, rather than something that is only activated during times of trouble.

Example: The Transformation of Maruti Suzuki

In the early 1980s, when Maruti Suzuki was first established in India, the company faced numerous challenges, including stiff competition from established players and the challenge of introducing a new brand in the Indian market. The crisis of establishing itself in a new market was turned into an opportunity by focusing on quality, customer satisfaction, and employee involvement.

Over the years, Maruti Suzuki embedded these lessons into its organizational culture. For instance, the practice of continuous improvement, or "Kaizen," became a core part of their operational strategy. This focus on quality and improvement has allowed Maruti Suzuki to maintain its position as the market leader in the Indian automobile industry for decades. The lessons learned during the early crisis became a permanent part of how the company operated, ensuring long-term success.

Developing Resilience as a Core Competency

Moving forward also involves developing resilience as a core competency within the organization. Resilience is the ability to bounce back from setbacks and adapt to changing circumstances—a crucial trait for any team that has been through a crisis.

Example: Infosys and Its Resilient Workforce

Infosys, one of India's leading IT services companies, has faced multiple challenges over the years, from leadership changes to market fluctuations. However, the company has consistently demonstrated resilience, which has become a defining characteristic of its workforce.

One example of this resilience is how Infosys managed the leadership transition in 2017, when Vishal Sikka resigned as CEO. The company quickly adapted to the situation, with a clear focus on maintaining stability and continuity. This was possible because Infosys had built resilience into its workforce—through leadership development programs, a strong organizational culture, and a focus on employee empowerment. As a result, Infosys was able to navigate the crisis without losing its momentum and continued to grow and innovate.

Continuous Learning and Adaptation

Another key aspect of moving forward is the commitment to continuous learning and adaptation. Organizations that have successfully navigated crises often have a culture of learning, where mistakes are viewed as opportunities for improvement, and there is a constant drive to adapt to new challenges.

Example: The Turnaround of HDFC Bank

In the late 1990s, HDFC Bank, under the leadership of Aditya Puri, faced intense competition as the Indian banking industry evolved rapidly. Recognizing the need for change, the bank embarked on a journey of continuous learning and adaptation, focusing on digital transformation. Early initiatives included launching internet and mobile banking services, which initially faced resistance from employees and technical challenges. To overcome these obstacles, HDFC Bank invested in training programs and fostered a culture of innovation, encouraging employees to embrace new technologies and learn from failures. The bank also prioritized customer feedback, using it to refine its digital offerings continually. This commitment to learning and adapting allowed HDFC Bank to improve customer satisfaction, enhance operational efficiency, and ultimately emerge as a leader in digital banking in India, setting a benchmark for innovation and customer-centricity in the industry.

Building Stronger Teams through Diversity and Inclusion

One of the lessons that often emerge from crises is the importance of diversity and inclusion in building strong teams. Diverse teams bring different perspectives and ideas to the table, which can be invaluable when navigating complex challenges. Moving forward, organizations should focus on building teams that are not only diverse in terms of gender, ethnicity, and background but also in terms of thought and experience.

Example: Tata Group's Commitment to Diversity

The Tata Group, one of India's largest and most respected conglomerates, has long recognized the value of diversity and inclusion. This commitment has been particularly evident in how the company has navigated crises.

For example, during the 2008 global financial crisis, the Tata Group faced significant challenges, including the need to manage its diverse portfolio of businesses across different industries and geographies. The company's diverse leadership team, with its range of experiences and perspectives, played a crucial role in navigating this crisis. By leveraging the strengths of its diverse workforce, Tata was able to make strategic decisions that helped the company emerge stronger from the crisis. Today, Tata continues to prioritize diversity and inclusion as key components of its organizational strategy, recognizing that these elements are critical to long-term success.

Institutionalizing Crisis Management Practices

To ensure that the benefits of crisis-driven strategies are sustained, organizations should institutionalize crisis management practices. This involves creating formal structures, processes, and policies that guide the organization's response to future crises.

Example: The Indian Space Research Organisation (ISRO)

ISRO is known for its ability to manage crisis effectively, whether it's a technical failure during a mission or budgetary constraints. One of the ways ISRO has institutionalized crisis management is by developing a robust project management framework that includes risk assessment, contingency planning, and post-crisis reviews.

For instance, after the failure of the GSLV (Geosynchronous Satellite Launch Vehicle) mission in 2010, ISRO conducted a thorough analysis of what went wrong, implemented corrective measures, and used the lessons learned to improve future missions. This approach paid off with the successful launch of the GSLV Mk III in 2014, which placed India's Mars Orbiter Mission into orbit. By institutionalizing these practices, ISRO has built a resilient organization capable of handling the inevitable challenges that come with space exploration.

Encouraging Innovation and Experimentation

Crises often force organizations to think outside the box and come up with innovative solutions to pressing problems. Moving forward, it's important to maintain this spirit of innovation and experimentation, even when the immediate crisis has passed.

Example: The Success of Amul's Innovative Marketing Strategies

Amul, India's largest dairy cooperative, has consistently demonstrated innovation in its marketing strategies, particularly during challenging times. For example, during the Covid-19 pandemic, when supply chains were disrupted, Amul quickly adapted by launching new products that catered to the needs of consumers who were staying at home. They also ramped up their digital marketing efforts, using social media to engage with customers and promote their products.

Amul's ability to innovate during a crisis is a reflection of its broader culture of experimentation and willingness to take risks. This approach has allowed Amul to stay relevant in a competitive market and continue to grow even during challenging times.

Fostering a Culture of Trust and Transparency

Trust and transparency are foundational to effective team building, especially during and after a crisis. Moving forward, organizations should focus on building a culture where trust is paramount, and transparency is the norm.

Example: The Turnaround of Satyam Computers

Satyam Computers, once a leading IT services company in India, faced a massive crisis in 2009 when it was revealed that the company's founder had been involved in a financial fraud. The crisis threatened to destroy the company, but under the leadership of the government-appointed board and the new CEO, C.P. Gurnani, Satyam (later rebranded as Tech Mahindra) managed to turn itself around.

One of the key factors in this turnaround was the focus on rebuilding trust with stakeholders—employees, customers, and investors. The new leadership team was transparent about the challenges the company faced and the steps being taken to address them. This openness helped restore confidence in the company and allowed it to recover from the crisis. Today, Tech Mahindra is a thriving company, thanks in large part to the culture of trust and transparency that was built during its most challenging times.

Preparing for the Future

Moving forward also means preparing for the future. Organizations need to be proactive in anticipating potential crises and developing strategies to address them before they occur. This involves scenario planning, risk management, and continuous monitoring of the internal and external environment.

Example: The Preparedness of the Indian Armed Forces

The Indian Armed Forces have long understood the importance of being prepared for future crises. Whether it's a natural disaster, a border conflict, or a cybersecurity threat, the armed forces invest heavily in scenario planning and preparedness exercises.

For example, the Indian Army's regular training exercises, such as Operation Vijay Prahar and Exercise Sudarshan Shakti, are designed to simulate real-world combat scenarios and test the readiness of the troops. These exercises not only prepare the forces for potential future conflicts but also help identify areas for improvement in strategy, tactics, and equipment. This focus on preparedness has enabled the Indian Armed Forces to respond effectively to a wide range of crises, both domestic and international.

The Role of Leadership in Moving Forward

Leadership plays a crucial role in moving forward after a crisis. Leaders set the tone for the organization, and their actions and decisions can have a profound impact on how well the organization recovers and grows. Moving forward, leaders must be able to inspire confidence, foster a positive organizational culture, and guide their teams through uncertainty.

Example: The Leadership of Indra Nooyi at PepsiCo

Indra Nooyi, the former CEO of PepsiCo, is often cited as an example of a leader who successfully guided her company through challenges and positioned it for long-term success. During her tenure, Nooyi faced multiple crises, including the challenge of balancing short-term financial performance with long-term sustainability goals.

One of Nooyi's key strategies was to focus on "Performance with Purpose," which aimed to align PepsiCo's business goals with broader social and environmental objectives. This approach not only helped the company navigate immediate challenges but also positioned it for future growth by addressing changing consumer preferences and societal expectations. Nooyi's leadership was instrumental in moving PepsiCo forward and ensuring that it remained a competitive and innovative company.

Conclusion: Sustaining the Momentum

Moving forward after a crisis is about more than just recovering; it's about sustaining the momentum and building on the progress that has been made. This requires a commitment to continuous improvement, a willingness to adapt to new challenges, and a focus on building strong, resilient teams.

As we have seen through the examples and stories shared in this chapter, organizations that successfully move forward after a crisis are those that embed the lessons learned into their culture, develop resilience as a core competency, and foster a spirit of innovation and trust. By doing so, they are not only able to navigate future crises more effectively but also position themselves for long-term success.

The journey of moving forward is ongoing. It requires constant vigilance, proactive planning, and a commitment to growth. But for those who are willing to put in the effort, the rewards are immense. By embracing the principles of crisis-driven team building and applying them consistently, organizations can build stronger, more resilient teams that are capable of achieving extraordinary results, no matter what challenges the future may hold.

Thank You

Dear Readers,

As this book comes to a close, I want to express my deepest gratitude to you, the reader. Your dedication to grow as a leader and commitment to your team is what makes a difference in times of crisis. It is your willingness to embrace challenges, learn from them, and guide your team through uncertainty that inspired the writing of this book.

Thank you for taking this journey with me. I hope the insights and stories shared here serve as a source of strength and inspiration as you continue to lead with courage, clarity, and compassion.

With heartfelt appreciation,

Ranabir Roy